FAITH FACTS

Answers to Catholic Questions

VOLUME II

FAITH FACTS

Answers to Catholic Questions

EMMAUS
ROAD
PUBLISHING

Leon J. Suprenant, Jr. and Philip C.L. Gray
Coeditors

Emmaus Road Publishing
827 North Fourth Street
Steubenville, Ohio 43952

Library of Congress Control Number: 2004101739
ISBN 1-931018-16-2

On the cover
Saint John Lateran Church, Rome
Photo by Beth Hart

Cover design and layout by
Beth Hart

Nihil obstat: Rev. James Dunfee, *Censor Librorum*
Imprimatur: ✠ R. Daniel Conlon, D.D., J.C.D., Ph.D.
Bishop of Steubenville
December 15, 2003

The *nihil obstat* and *imprimatur* are official declarations
that a book or pamphlet is free of doctrinal or moral error.
No implication is contained therein that those who have
granted the *nihil obstat* and *imprimatur* agree with
the contents, opinions, or statements expressed.

Contents

Life Issues

Marriage Issues

Biblical Apologetics

Spiritual Counterfeits?

In his apostolic exhortation *Christifideles Laici*, Pope John Paul II writes: "The situation today points to an ever-increasing urgency for *a doctrinal* formation of the lay faithful, not simply in a better understanding which is natural to faith's dynamism but also in enabling them to 'give a reason for their hoping' in view of the world and its grave and complex problems. Therefore, a systematic approach to *catechesis*, geared to age and the diverse situations of life, is an absolute necessity."[1]

In response to the Holy Father's call for the doctrinal formation of the laity, Catholics United for the Faith (CUF) offers a variety of services to meet the needs of today's Catholic. These services include the award winning *Lay Witness* magazine, the *Faith and Life* catechism series, and dynamic Catholic Bible studies and lay formation materials published through Emmaus Road, CUF's book publishing division. CUF also offers national and regional conferences, retreats and programs, and a toll-free Catholic hotline (1-800-MY-FAITH).

One of our services is the production of tracts known as FAITH FACTS. Each FAITH FACT sets forth clearly, concisely, and without "spin" the teachings and practices of the Catholic Church. They rely principally on Scripture and the *Catechism of the Catholic Church*, but additional authoritative sources are provided in the text.

This is the second collection of FAITH FACTS. Volume I, also available through Emmaus Road Publishing, was released in 1999, and its popularity encouraged us to publish this second volume.

The FAITH FACTS in this new book, and FAITH FACTS generally, are reflective of the accumulated research and experience

---

[1] Pope John Paul II, On the Vocation and the Mission of the Lay Faithful in the Church and in the World *Christifideles Laici* (December 30, 1988), no. 60, emphasis in original.

of the CUF apostolate, which is now celebrating its thirty-fifth year in service of Jesus Christ and His Church. As such, many people contributed to this project. In addition to my talented coeditor, Philip Gray, I want to acknowledge the efforts of our staff members, past and present, who have contributed to this project, especially full-time Catholic apologists, Eric Stoutz, Tom Nash, and David Utsler, whose labors are reflected on these pages. I also thank Helen Valois, who wrote the original version of *Debunking the Overpopulation Myth*, chapter 2 in this volume.

Lastly, I would like to add a word of thanks to the tens of thousands of CUF members through the decades, whose prayers, sacrifices, fidelity, and encouragement have made possible the vital work of our apostolate. I have been blessed to spend time with many of them, and I believe them to be numbered among the unsung heroes of our time. May our Lord bless their unwavering commitment to "support, defend, and advance the efforts of the teaching Church."

LEON J. SUPRENANT

Old Testament
Gen./Genesis
Ex./Exodus
Lev./Leviticus
Num./Numbers
Deut./Deuteronomy
Josh./Joshua
Judg./Judges
Ruth/Ruth
1 Sam./1 Samuel
2 Sam./2 Samuel
1 Kings/1 Kings
2 Kings/2 Kings
1 Chron./1 Chronicles
2 Chron./2 Chronicles
Ezra/Ezra
Neh./Nehemiah
Tob./Tobit
Jud./Judith
Esther/Esther
Job/Job
Ps./Psalms
Prov./Proverbs
Eccles./Ecclesiastes
Song/Song of Solomon
Wis./Wisdom
Sir./Sirach (Ecclesiasticus)
Is./Isaiah
Jer./Jeremiah

Lam./Lamentations
Bar./Baruch
Ezek./Ezekiel
Dan./Daniel
Hos./Hosea
Joel/Joel
Amos/Amos
Obad./Obadiah
Jon./Jonah
Mic./Micah
Nahum/Nahum
Hab./Habakkuk
Zeph./Zephaniah
Hag./Haggai
Zech./Zechariah
Mal./Malachi
1 Mac./1 Maccabees
2 Mac./2 Maccabees

New Testament
Mt./Matthew
Mk./Mark
Lk./Luke
Jn./John
Acts/Acts of the Apostles
Rom./Romans
1 Cor./1 Corinthians
2 Cor./2 Corinthians
Gal./Galatians

Eph./Ephesians
Phil./Philippians
Col./Colossians
1 Thess./1 Thessalonians
2 Thess./2 Thessalonians
1 Tim./1 Timothy
2 Tim./2 Timothy
Tit./Titus
Philem./Philemon
Heb./Hebrews
Jas./James
1 Pet./1 Peter
2 Pet./2 Peter
1 Jn./1 John
2 Jn./2 John
3 Jn./3 John
Jude/Jude
Rev./Revelation (Apocalypse)

Chapter 1

WHO ART IN HEAVEN
THE DWELLING PLACE OF GOD

What is heaven? Where is it?

Heaven is "a living, personal relationship with the Holy Trinity. It is our meeting with the Father which takes place in the risen Christ through the communion of the Holy Spirit."[1] It is the fulfillment of God's desire to be one with each man as God is one with Himself in the Trinity (cf. Jn. 17:20–24).

The Church does not identify a specific place for heaven, such as in the clouds, but does affirm that heaven is union with God, face to face, without the mediation of any creature (cf. Catechism, nos. 1023–29).

Because of our limited understanding, no amount of description will provide a satisfying understanding of the sublime reality of heaven. Historically, various theologians have described heaven as both a place and a state of being. However, no one can capture the reality and essence of heaven until he has experienced it personally. As Saint Paul wrote, "What no eye has seen, nor ear heard, nor the heart of man conceived, what God has prepared for those who love him" (1 Cor. 2:9).

Time and Space: The First Frontiers

Time and space are created things. As noted in Genesis 1:1, "In the beginning God created the heavens and the earth." There was a moment at which time began. This moment was an act of creation by God, Who is not bound by time. At that moment, God also created space, namely the heavens and the

---

[1] Pope John Paul II, General Audience (July 21, 1999), no. 4.

earth. Though they are two separate creatures, time and space complement each other. Space was created within time, and creatures of space (e.g., sun, moon, and stars) provide a telling of time.

When considering the topic of heaven, we should remember that during our earthly lives, we experience time and space simultaneously. However, as separate and distinct created realities, they need not exist together.

God created man within the limits of time and space. These limits have their benefits. When we sin, we have time to repent and turn to God for mercy. Because of time, we have the opportunity to change our ways. We depend on the experiences of time and space to grow in knowledge and understanding. We do not simply know things; we learn them by experiences with other creatures. When we express our knowledge and thoughts, we do so according to the limits of our experience.

Say What?

Language is a powerful symbol that man uses in order to express himself. By use of language, other signs and symbols are explained. Yet language falls short of expressing realities we do not fully understand. Everyone experiences this lack of comprehension: On one occasion or another, we grapple with the right words to use when describing an experience or idea. We simply do not know what to say.

Heaven is one of those realities we do not fully understand. It is not limited to time and space as we are. As a result, none of our experiences with other creatures on earth can fully reveal the nature of heaven, nor can our languages or imaginations describe it perfectly (cf. 1 Cor. 2:9).

When describing heaven, man traditionally has taken one of two approaches: He describes heaven either as a state of being or as a place, depending upon whether he considers the characteristics of God or the characteristics of man.

Where Are You Going?

God is eternal and omnipresent. He is not bound by time or space. He existed before their creation. Because heaven existed as the dwelling place of God before time began, it must be eternal as well. This leaves us with two possibilities. If we consider heaven as a created space, it must be a space "eternally created" by the very presence of God. This concept of "eternal creation" makes no sense to our human understanding.[2] If heaven is not a creature, then it is simply God's eternal presence. In either case, heaven would be both eternal and omnipresent, bound by neither time nor space. If heaven is omnipresent, can we really call it a place? With this line of reasoning, it is easy to see that heaven is far different from any place comprehensible to man on earth.

Explaining heaven as a state of being eliminates the confusion between created space bound by time, and created space apart from time. Explaining heaven as a state of being appeals to the characteristics of God, particularly His eternal and omnipresent nature. Our inheritance of heaven as a state of being, and not a place per se, is understood as our fullness of communion with God. Traditionally, this fullness of communion is known as the *beatific vision*, the contemplation of God in His heavenly glory.

Heaven, however, must contain space because it contains the glorified body of Christ (cf. Mk. 16:19; Lk. 24:51), as well as the bodies of Enoch (cf. Gen. 5:24), Moses (cf. Jude 9), Elijah (cf. 2 Kings 2:9–12), and the Blessed Virgin Mary (cf. Rev. 12:1). At the end of time, it will contain the glorified bodies of all the saints (cf. Catechism, nos. 988–1019). Its reality, however, is not a place bound by time and space as we know it, and this kind of reality is incomprehensible to us. Its spatial reality is a reality of God's glory, not a reality of the created world.

Union with God

In magisterial documents, the Church neither states where heaven is nor defines it solely as a state of being. The Church does describe what happens in heaven, namely, union with God and with all His angels and saints (cf. Jn. 17:20–26; Catechism, nos. 1023–24). Though in union with God, man does not lose

---

[2] Some theologians use the term "aeviternal" to explain this concept. Cf. Frank Sheed, *Theology and Sanity* (New York: Sheed & Ward, 1946), 115–16, 297–99.

his distinct nature and identity (cf. Catechism, no. 1025). He remains human, but becomes fully human in Christ, as intended by God. This perfect union with God and transformation in Christ is what is most important, not arguments about whether heaven is a place or state of being.

> By this Constitution which is to remain in force forever, we, with apostolic authority, define the following: According to the general disposition of God, the souls of all the saints . . . have been, are and will be with Christ in heaven, in the heavenly kingdom and paradise, joined to the company of the holy angels. Since the passion and death of the Lord Jesus Christ, these souls have seen and see the divine essence with an intuitive vision and even face to face, without the mediation of any creature by way of object of vision; rather the divine essence immediately manifests itself to them, plainly, clearly and openly, and in this vision they enjoy the divine essence. Moreover, by this vision and enjoyment the souls of those who have already died are truly blessed and have eternal life and rest . . . and will continue without any interruption and without end until the last Judgment and from then on forever.[3]

The Magisterium does not favor one theological approach over another. However, it does emphasize what happens in heaven, and uses common language to help describe different characteristics of heaven. In his edict *Benedictus Deus* (quoted above), Pope Benedict XII uses the phrase "will be with Christ in heaven" to describe the destiny of the faithful departed. "In" can refer to a place or a state of being without favoring one over the other. More recently, Pope John Paul II stated, "Today, personalist language is better suited to describing the state of happiness and peace we will enjoy in our definitive communion with God."[4] While he uses the term "state," he does not limit the term to "state of being," "state of mind," or "state of

---

[3] Pope Benedict XII, Constitution on the Beatific Vision of God *Benedictus Deus* (January 29, 1336), in J. Neuner and J. Dupuis, ed., *The Christian Faith in the Doctrinal Documents of the Catholic Church* (Westminster, Md.: Christian Classics, 1975), 623–24.

[4] Pope John Paul II, General Audience (July 21, 1999), no. 4.

body." To explain the concept further, he quotes the Catechism: "The life of the blessed consists in the full and perfect possession of the fruits of the redemption accomplished by Christ. He makes partners in his heavenly glorification those who have believed in him and remained faithful to his will. Heaven is the blessed community of all who are perfectly incorporated into Christ" (no. 1026).

As Saint Augustine wrote, "You made us for Yourself, and our hearts are restless until they rest in You."[5] Heaven fulfills the desire of our hearts for God. Our lives on earth must be directed to seeking that perfect union with God that He meant for us from the beginning. When we reach that heavenly beatitude, our hearts will be filled with an intense love and joy that can only be described as God Himself.

Heaven on Earth

Many have tried to compare earthly experiences to heavenly realities. In Sacred Scripture, one of the most compelling signs of heaven's glory is marriage, the union of a man and woman in a covenant of love with God (cf. Gen. 1:26–27; Rev. 21:1–4). As intended from the beginning, marriage involves a total and free sacrifice of self for love of the other in the love of God. When this love is returned by the spouse, the mutual love of both brings unspeakable joy for life and hope for the future. The ecstasies shared by the couple in their love foreshadow the ecstasies of heaven and our union with God. For this reason, Saint Paul, when writing about marriage, could say, "This is a great mystery, and I mean in reference to Christ and the church" (Eph. 5:32).

In addition to marriage, the liturgies of the Church and the other sacraments foreshadow the realities of heaven's glories. This is particularly true of the celebration of the Mass and the Sacrament of the Holy Eucharist. The liturgy of the Mass draws from the elaborate and beautiful images given to us in the Book of Revelation, where Saint John describes heaven and the

---

[5] Saint Augustine of Hippo, *Confessions*, bk. 1, chap. 1, no. 1, in William A. Jurgens, trans., *Faith of the Early Fathers*, *vol. 3* (Collegeville, Minn.: The Liturgical Press, 1979), 56.

praises of the angels and saints before God (cf. Rev. 4–5). When we participate in the celebration of the Mass, we are mysteriously drawn into the unending praises of God in heaven. We participate in temporary worship that is outside of time. Because the Holy Eucharist is the Body and Blood of Jesus, our Lord and God, when we receive this Sacrament, we experience the greatest physical and spiritual union with God on earth. Thus we mysteriously receive a foretaste of the union God intends for us in heaven (cf. Catechism, nos. 1000, 1402–05).

Our participation in the liturgies and sacraments of the Church are nothing less than our participation in the communion of saints. As the saints and angels worship before God in heaven, we participate on earth in their glorious praise of His name. The glory given the saints in heaven is our hope as we yearn for God during our earthly exile. God has given us on earth a glimpse of heavenly realities so that we may not lose heart. Let us find in our marriages, families, and daily work the encouragement to keep our focus on God, until that day when we shall see Him face to face.

_____*SideBar*___

One Day in the Life of a Saint in Heaven

For by reason of the fact that those in heaven are more closely united with Christ, they establish the whole Church more firmly in holiness, lend nobility to the worship which the Church offers to God here on earth and in many ways contribute to its greater edification. For after they have been received into their heavenly home and are present to the Lord, through Him and with Him and in Him they do not cease to intercede with the Father for us, showing forth the merits which they won on earth through the one Mediator between God and man, serving God in all things and filling up in their flesh those things which are lacking of the sufferings of Christ for His Body which is the Church. Thus by their brotherly interest our weakness is greatly strengthened.[6]

---

[6] Second Vatican Council, Dogmatic Constitution on the Church *Lumen Gentium* (November 21, 1964), no. 49.

Questions for Reflection
or Group Discussion

1. How is heaven described in the Bible?

2. What makes heaven a difficult reality to understand?

3. How can I live my life in anticipation of heaven's glories?

4. What circumstances and events do I encounter every day that remind me of heaven?

Chapter 2

WHO KNOWS?
THE HUMAN KNOWLEDGE OF CHRIST

What does the Church teach about Christ's human knowledge?

The constant teaching of the Church is that Christ, in His human intellect, from the moment of His conception, knew all things that a created intellect could know.

This issue points to the great mystery of the Incarnation, when, in the fullness of time, God took on human nature (cf. Jn. 1:14; Gal. 4:4–5). In doing so, our God, in the Person of Jesus Christ, united Himself in some fashion with every human person. As we consider the mystery of Christ's being fully human and fully divine, we are filled with wonder and joy. For God is truly with us; He has visited His people (cf. Is. 7:14; Mt. 1:23; Lk. 7:16), offering salvation to all the nations.

God Only Knows

The Church affirms that human nature was assumed and not absorbed in the Incarnation.[1] In His Person, Christ is true God *and* true man, not some mixture of the human and divine (cf. Catechism, no. 464). In trying to come to grips with this truth, many great minds throughout history have fallen into error by embracing only part of this magnificent reality. Many people today, in rightly affirming Christ's humanity, have failed to leave room for the complementary truth that Christ is also fully divine. Indeed, "today, because of the rationalism found in so much of contemporary culture, it is above all faith in the divinity of Christ that has become problematic."[2] Within

---

[1] Cf. Athanasian Creed; available from http://www.newadvent.org/cathen/02033b.htm.
[2] Pope John Paul II, Apostolic Letter at the Close of the Great Jubilee of the Year 2000 *Novo Millennio Ineunte* (January 6, 2001), no. 22.

this context, we examine Christ's human knowledge. It is legitimate to ask how God could at the same time be one like us (cf. Heb. 4:15) and yet know everything. However, the answer to this question must be faithful to the data of divine revelation as consistently taught by the Church.

We must confess, as the Church has done consistently throughout her history, that Jesus Christ is fully human. This truth is summarized in the Catechism, which in turn quotes Vatican II, *Gaudium et Spes*, no. 22: "The Son of God . . . worked with human hands; he thought with a human mind. He acted with a human will, and with a human heart he loved. Born of the Virgin Mary, he has truly been made one of us, like to us in all things except sin" (no. 470).

Yet, because He is also fully divine, Christ has a divine intellect as well as a human intellect. His human intellect of itself is limited, because it does not have the full comprehension of divinity; that is something only His divine intellect possesses. Yet the consensus of Fathers, popes, and doctors of the Church is that His human intellect has constant and habitual knowledge of all things that a created intellect can know.

A survey of magisterial statements demonstrates this point. In the year 600, Pope Saint Gregory I (the Great) affirmed that anyone who interprets Mark 13:32 to mean that Christ did not know the day or the hour of judgment is necessarily a Nestorian; that is, one who erroneously holds that Christ is two distinct persons, one human and one divine, such that He did not know the day or the hour only as a *human* person. The pope explained the correct meaning of this passage, teaching that Christ "knew indeed in the nature of His humanity the day and the hour of the judgment, but still it was not from the nature of His humanity that He knew it. . . . The day, then, and the hour of judgment He knows as God and man, but for this reason, that God is man."[3] In other words, Christ as man knew the day and the hour, but only because He is God, which informed His human nature, and not by virtue of His human nature alone.

---

[3] Saint Gregory the Great, *Epistle 39 to Eulogius, Patriarch of Alexandria*, in *Nicene and Post-Nicene Fathers*, 2d ser., vol. 13, ed. Philip Schaff and Henry Wace (Peabody, Mass.: Hendrickson Publishers, 1994), 48.

Magisterial Pronouncements

In 1907, Pope Saint Pius X rejected the Modernist proposition that "Christ did not always possess the consciousness of His Messianic dignity."[4] In 1918, the Holy Office condemned the propositions that Christ, while on earth, did not have the knowledge that the blessed enjoy in heaven and that He was ignorant of some things a created intellect could potentially know. In 1943, Pope Pius XII affirmed that "hardly was [Christ] conceived in the womb of the Mother of God, when He began to enjoy the Beatific Vision, and in that vision all the members of His Mystical Body were continually and unceasingly present to Him, and He embraced them with His redeeming love."[5]

In His humanity, the Lord grew, learned, had human emotions, prayed, and suffered. Nonetheless, all these human attributes belong to the Divine Person Whose humanity this is. Thus, in His humanity, in His human mind and human will, Jesus of Nazareth was (and is) aware of His own divine identity. As the Catechism puts it: "Christ, being true God and true man, has a human intellect and will, perfectly attuned and subject to his divine intellect and divine will, which he has in common with the Father and the Holy Spirit" (no. 482). Indeed, "[b]y its union to the divine wisdom in the person of the Word incarnate, Christ enjoyed in his human knowledge the fullness of understanding of the eternal plans he had come to reveal. What he admitted to not knowing in this area, he elsewhere declared himself not sent to reveal [cf. Mk. 13:32; Acts 1:7]" (Catechism, no. 474). This means that Jesus knew everything as God, but only disclosed what He was sent to reveal by the Father.

God-Man with a Mission

Included in the human knowledge of the incarnate God was the very purpose of His coming: to die for the sins of all (Christ's "redemptive passion was the very reason for his Incarnation" [Catechism, no. 607]). "Jesus' violent death was

---

[4] Pope Saint Pius X, Syllabus Condemning the Errors of the Modernists *Lamentabili Sane* (July 3, 1907), no. 35.
[5] Pope Pius XII, Encyclical on the Mystical Body of Christ *Mystici Corporis Christi* (June 29, 1943), no. 75.

not the result of chance in an unfortunate coincidence of circumstances, but is part of the mystery of God's plan."
(Catechism, no. 599). United with the Father, Christ gives
Himself up to death for us, so "that he could say in our name
from the cross: 'My God, my God, why have you forsaken me?'
[Mk. 15:34; Ps. 22:2; cf. Jn. 8:29]" (Catechism, no. 603). We
should note that the cry is said "in our name"; Jesus Himself
never knows abandonment by the Father.

And what about Luke 2:52, which plainly declares that
Christ grew "in wisdom and in stature"? According to Saint
Thomas Aquinas, a real progress was not possible for Christ in
His beatific knowledge and His infused knowledge, as these
contained from the very beginning all things that could be
known by a created intellect. However, Christ as man did
have experiential knowledge, but this knowledge would have
been new not in content, *but only in the manner of acquisition.*
The fact that Christ grew "in wisdom and in stature" does not
mean that He gained new knowledge that He didn't have
before, but rather that He gained in a new way knowledge that
He already had.[6]

Pope John Paul II explains the mystery this way:

> However valid it may be to maintain that, because of the
> human condition which made him grow "in wisdom and in
> stature, and in favor with God and man" (Lk. 2:52), his human
> awareness of his own mystery would also have progressed to its
> fullest expression in his glorified humanity, there is no doubt
> that already in his historical existence Jesus was aware of his
> identity as the Son of God. John emphasizes this to the point
> of affirming that it was ultimately because of this awareness
> that Jesus was rejected and condemned: they sought to kill
> him "because he not only broke the sabbath but also called
> God his Father, making himself equal with God" (Jn. 5:18). In
> Gethsemane and on Golgotha Jesus' human awareness will be

---

[6] Cf. Saint Thomas Aquinas, *Summa Theologiae*, IIIa, q. 12, art. 2.; available from
http://www.newadvent.org/summa/401202.htm.

put to the supreme test. But not even the drama of his Passion and Death will be able to shake his serene certainty of being the Son of the heavenly Father.[7]

Questions for Reflection or Group Discussion

1. What are some contemporary obstacles to faith in Christ's divinity?

2. Based on what I have just read, how would I respond to the following: "Christ, one like us in all things but sin, Who 'grew in wisdom and grace' during His formative years in Nazareth, only gradually became aware that He was truly the Messiah"?

3. What does the Incarnation teach me about my dignity as a human person? (See Catechism, no. 1701.)

---

[7] Pope John Paul II, *Novo Millennio Ineunte*, no. 24.

ALL ABOARD!
WITHOUT THE CHURCH THERE IS NO SALVATION

What does the Catholic Church mean by the phrase, "Outside the Church there is no salvation" (extra ecclesiam nulla salus)?

All salvation comes through Jesus Christ, the one Savior of the world (cf. Acts 4:12). His Holy Spirit dispenses the graces of salvation through His Body, the Church. Christ told the apostles, "He who hears you hears me, and he who rejects you rejects me, and he who rejects me rejects him who sent me" (Lk. 10:16). As stated in Vatican II's Dogmatic Constitution on the Church, "Basing itself upon Sacred Scripture and Tradition, [this holy Council] teaches that the Church, now sojourning on earth as an exile, is necessary for salvation."[1] Quoting from various documents of Vatican II and Pope Paul VI, the Catechism explains:

> As sacrament, the Church is Christ's instrument. "She is taken up by him also as the instrument for the salvation of all," "the universal sacrament of salvation," by which Christ is "at once manifesting and actualizing the mystery of God's love for men [LG 9 § 2, 48 § 2; GS 45 § 1]." The Church "is the visible plan of God's love for humanity," because God desires "that the whole human race may become one People of God, form one Body of Christ, and be built up into one temple of the Holy Spirit [Paul VI, June 22, 1973; AG 7 § 2; cf. LG 17]" (no. 776; see also nos. 846–48).

There are two principal errors in understanding the Church's teaching on *extra ecclesiam nulla salus*. Some reject this teaching

---

[1] Second Vatican Council, Dogmatic Constitution on the Church *Lumen Gentium* (November 21, 1964), no. 14.

as arrogant and outdated. Others interpret this statement to condemn all those who are not visibly united to the Catholic Church. To come to the proper understanding of this teaching, we must examine it within the context of divine revelation and Church history. This examination will reveal that the phrase was not formulated to express who would go to heaven and who would go to hell, for only God can judge that. Rather, the phrase expresses an understanding of the Church in relation to her role in the salvation of the world.

Scriptural Foundations

According to the Gospel of Mark, Jesus appeared to the eleven after the Resurrection and gave them the commission, "Go into all the world and preach the gospel to the whole creation. He who believes and is baptized will be saved; but he who does not believe will be condemned" (Mk. 16:15–16). In order to accept or reject the Gospel, each person must have it preached to him. If acceptance or rejection of the truth were based on private revelations given to each man, woman, and child, there would be no need for Christ to commission the apostles to preach the Gospel. Jesus desired to reveal Himself through His Body, the Church. While this passage condemns those who reject the truth, it does not condemn those who have not had the truth offered to them as Christ intends.

The New Testament clearly teaches that salvation is a gift offered by God in various ways to all men. Adam, Abel, and Enoch lived between the first sin and the covenant of Noah. They were bound by original sin, yet all of them are considered to be in heaven. Enoch did not even die, but was taken to God before death (cf. Heb. 11:4–5). These men were neither baptized nor circumcised, but they were nonetheless saved.

When the Gentile centurion came to Jesus in Capernaum and asked for the healing of his servant, our Lord agreed to go to his home, but the centurion said, "Lord, I am not worthy to have you come under my roof; but only say the word, and my servant will be healed" (Mt. 8:8). Jesus replied, "Truly, I say to you, not even in Israel have I found such faith. I tell you, many will come from east and west and sit at table with Abraham, Isaac, and Jacob in the kingdom of heaven, while the sons of the kingdom will be thrown into the outer darkness; there men will weep and gnash their teeth" (Mt. 8:10–12).

Jesus makes a clear distinction between those who are sons of the Kingdom (that is, those who have knowledge of the faith and have accepted it) and those who are not. He includes in the Kingdom of heaven many of those who are not sons of the Kingdom. Jesus offers us grace through His Incarnation, and His presence is known through His Body, the Church, which carries on the work of Christ here on earth. Those to whom the Church has not preached the Good News will be judged by God in a manner known to Him alone and tempered by His mercy. As Saint Paul explains, "When Gentiles who have not the law do by nature what the law requires, they are a law to themselves, even though they do not have the law. They show that what the law requires is written on their hearts, while their conscience also bears witness and their conflicting thoughts accuse or perhaps excuse them on that day when, according to my gospel, God judges the secrets of men by Christ Jesus" (Rom. 2:14–16).

Sacred Tradition

Many people who claim that God restricts salvation to baptized Catholics cite the Fathers of the Church to prove their assertions. While space does not allow an exhaustive analysis of the Fathers, there are several points we must keep in mind. First, the Fathers must be understood in the context of their writings, rather than in the context of the one quoting them. The majority of the Fathers who wrote on this topic were concerned about those who had once believed or had heard the truth, but now rejected it. Many of them believed the entire world had heard the Gospel. Their words were not directed at those who, by no fault of their own, did not know the Gospel of Christ.

The Fathers do affirm the inherent danger of deliberately rejecting the Church. For example, Saint Ignatius of Antioch wrote at the beginning of the second century, "Do not err, my brethren. If any man follows him that makes a schism in the Church, he shall not inherit the kingdom of God."[2] In the third

---

[2] Saint Ignatius of Antioch, *Epistle to the Philadelphians*, chap. 3, in *Ante-Nicene Fathers*, vol. 1, ed. Alexander Roberts and James Donaldson (Peabody, Mass.: Hendrickson Publishers, 1994), 80.

century, Saint Cyprian of Carthage wrote, "Whoever is separated from the Church and is joined to an adulteress [a schismatic church], is separated from the promises of the Church; nor can he who forsakes the Church of Christ attain to the rewards of Christ. He is a stranger; he is profane; he is an enemy."[3] In the fourth century, Saint Jerome wrote, "Heretics bring sentence upon themselves since they by their own choice withdraw from the Church, a withdrawal which, since they are aware of it, constitutes damnation."[4]

On the other hand, many of the Fathers did write about those who were invincibly ignorant of the Gospel—that is, those who, through no fault of their own, had not had the opportunity to hear the Gospel. The Fathers believed that salvation was open to them, even if in a mysterious way. The Fathers recognized that the natural law of justice and virtue is written on the hearts of all men. Those who respect this law respect the Lawgiver, though they do not know Him. As Saint Justin Martyr wrote in the second century, "We have been taught that Christ is the first-born of God, and we have declared above that He is the Word of whom every race of men were partakers; and those who lived reasonably are Christians, even though they have been thought atheists; as, among the Greeks, Socrates and Heraclitus, and men like them . . . they who lived before Christ, and lived without reason, were wicked and hostile to Christ, and slew those who lived reasonably. But who, through the power of the Word, according to the will of God the Father and Lord of all, He was born of a virgin as a man, and was named Jesus, and was crucified, and died, and rose again, and ascended into heaven, an intelligent man will be able to comprehend from what has been already so largely said."[5]

---

[3] Saint Cyprian of Carthage, *Treatise I. On the Unity of the Church*, no. 6, in *Ante-Nicene Fathers*, vol. 5, ed. Alexander Roberts and James Donaldson (Peabody, Mass.: Hendrickson Publishers, 1994), 423.

[4] Saint Jerome, *Commentary on Titus*, 3:10–11.

[5] Saint Justin Martyr, *First Apology*, chap. 46, in *Ante-Nicene Fathers*, vol. 1, ed. Alexander Roberts and James Donaldson (Peabody, Mass.: Hendrickson Publishers, 1994), 178.

Similarly, Saint Clement of Alexandria wrote in the third century, "Accordingly, before the advent of the Lord, philosophy was necessary to the Greeks for righteousness. And now it becomes conducive to piety . . . For this was a schoolmaster to bring 'the Hellenic mind,' as the law, the Hebrews, 'to Christ.'"[6] Origen, writing in the same era, added, "[T]here was never a time when God did not wish to make men live righteous lives; but He continually evinced His care for the improvement of the rational animal, by affording him occasions for the exercise of virtue. For in every generation the wisdom of God, passing into those souls which it ascertains to be holy, converts them into friends and prophets of God."[7] In the fifth century, Saint Augustine wrote, "[W]hen we speak of within and without in relation to the Church, it is the position of the heart that we must consider, not that of the body since all who are within in heart are saved in the unity of the ark."[8]

Magisterial Pronouncements

Throughout the history of the Church, the Magisterium has accepted and synthesized these teachings. Recognizing that God will judge our hearts according to the gifts we have received, invincible ignorance tempers divine justice. Those who have knowledge of the truth are expected to accept it. Those who have not been given this gift will be judged according to the law written on their hearts. Two noteworthy examples of this position are found in Pope Boniface VIII's bull *Unam Sanctam* and Blessed Pius IX's encyclical *Quanto conficiamur moerore*.

---

[6] Saint Clement of Alexandria, *Miscellanies*, bk. 1, chap. 5, in *Ante-Nicene Fathers*, vol. 2, ed. Alexander Roberts and James Donaldson (Peabody, Mass.: Hendrickson Publishers, 1994), 305.
[7] Origen, *Against Celsus*, bk. 4, chap. 7, in *Ante-Nicene Fathers*, vol. 4, ed. Alexander Roberts and James Donaldson (Peabody, Mass.: Hendrickson Publishers, 1994), 500.
[8] Saint Augustine, *On Baptism against the Donatists*, bk. V, chap. 28, no. 39, trans. J. R. King, in *Nicene and Post-Nicene Fathers*, 1st ser., vol. 4, ed. Philip Schaff (Peabody, Mass.: Hendrickson Publishers, 1994), 478.

Boniface VIII wrote about the nature of the Church and the supremacy of the pope. He did not write about the damnation of those who have never heard the Gospel. After expressing the truth that there is only one Lord, one faith, one Baptism, and one Church, he explained that the supreme authority of the pope is both temporal and spiritual. He then concluded, "[W]e declare, state and define that it is absolutely necessary for the salvation of all men that they submit to the Roman Pontiff."[9] This is not a statement demanding that everyone know of the supremacy of the pope to be saved, but rather is a truthful claim that the pope has authority from God as the legitimate successor of Saint Peter, to whom our Lord entrusted the keys of the kingdom.

Blessed Pius IX clearly expressed the full teaching over a century ago. His writing distinguishes between those who are invincibly ignorant and those who have willfully separated themselves from the Catholic Church:

> We all know that those who suffer from invincible ignorance with regard to our holy religion, if they carefully keep the precepts of the natural law which have been written by God in the hearts of all men, if they are prepared to obey God, and if they lead a virtuous and dutiful life, can, by the power of divine light and grace, attain eternal life. For God, who knows completely the minds and souls, the thoughts and habits of all men, will not permit, in accord with His infinite goodness and mercy, anyone who is not guilty of a voluntary fault to suffer eternal punishment.

> However, also well known is the Catholic dogma that no one can be saved outside the Catholic Church, and that those who obstinately oppose the authority of the definitions of the Church, and who stubbornly remain separated from the unity of the Church and from the successor of Peter, the Roman

---

[9] Pope Boniface VIII, Bull *Unam Sanctam* (November 18, 1302), in J. Neuner and J. Dupuis, ed., *The Christian Faith in the Doctrinal Documents of the Catholic Church* (Westminster, Md.: Christian Classics, 1975), 210–11.

Pontiff, to whom the Saviour has entrusted the care of His vineyard, cannot obtain salvation.[10]

Sacrament of Salvation

A century later at Vatican II, an expression of the authentic Magisterium, the college of bishops further explained this doctrine in the context of Christocentric sacramental theology at Vatican II. Echoing the words of Saint Paul, the council described the Church as the Spouse and Body of Christ. Jesus is one with His Spouse, the Church (cf. Eph. 5:32). The two form the one Body of Christ visible on earth. Christ is the Head, and He ministers through His Body as the sacrament of salvation. To whom does He minister? Both to His Body and to those apart from the Body, that he might draw all men to Himself.[11] In this way, the Church dispenses to all men the graces of salvation won by Christ. Those who knowingly reject these graces are lost. Those who accept them are saved. Those who do not have the opportunity to accept these graces can be saved because of the presence of the Church in the world (cf. 1 Cor. 7:12–16). If they are saved, they are saved through the Church without their knowledge of these graces. The Council teaches:

> This Sacred Council wishes to turn its attention firstly to the Catholic faithful. Basing itself upon Sacred Scripture and Tradition, it teaches that the Church, now sojourning on earth as an exile, is necessary for salvation. Christ, present to us in His Body, which is the Church, is the one Mediator and the unique way of salvation. In explicit terms He Himself affirmed the necessity of faith and baptism and thereby affirmed also the necessity of the Church, for through baptism as through a door men enter the Church. Whosoever, therefore, knowing that the Catholic Church was made necessary by Christ, would refuse to enter or to remain in it, could not be saved.

---

[10] Blessed Pius IX, Encyclical Letter to the Bishops of Italy on Salvation in the Church *Quanto conficiamur moerore* (August 10, 1863), in *The Christian Faith in the Doctrinal Documents of the Catholic Church*, 217–18.

[11] Cf. Second Vatican Council, *Lumen Gentium*, nos. 6–7, 9, 13.

They are fully incorporated in the society of the Church who, possessing the Spirit of Christ accept her entire system and all the means of salvation given to her, and are united with her as part of her visible bodily structure and through her with Christ, who rules her through the Supreme Pontiff and the bishops. The bonds which bind men to the Church in a visible way are profession of faith, the sacraments, and ecclesiastical government and communion. He is not saved, however, who, though part of the body of the Church, does not persevere in charity. He remains indeed in the bosom of the Church, but, as it were, only in a "bodily" manner and not "in his heart." All the Church's children should remember that their exalted status is to be attributed not to their own merits but to the special grace of Christ. If they fail moreover to respond to that grace in thought, word and deed, not only shall they not be saved but they will be the more severely judged.[12]

Elsewhere, the Council Fathers teach:

Moreover, some and even very many of the significant elements and endowments which together go to build up and give life to the Church itself, can exist outside the visible boundaries of the Catholic Church: the written word of God; the life of grace; faith, hope and charity, with the other interior gifts of the Holy Spirit, and visible elements too. All of these, which come from Christ and lead back to Christ, belong by right to the one Church of Christ. . . . It follows that the separated Churches and Communities as such, though we believe them to be deficient in some respects, have been by no means deprived of significance and importance in the mystery of salvation. For the Spirit of Christ has not refrained from using them as means of salvation which derive their efficacy from the very fullness of grace and truth entrusted to the Church.[13]

---

[12] Second Vatican Council, *Lumen Gentium*, no. 14.
[13] Second Vatican Council, Decree on Ecumenism *Unitatis Redintegratio* (November 21, 1964), no. 3.

Come Aboard!

This teaching of Christ and His Church is not meant to allow indifferentism or exclusivism. Baptism and unity with the Catholic Church provide the only assurance of salvation, but not the only means of salvation. *"God has bound salvation to the sacrament of Baptism, but he himself is not bound by his sacraments"* (Catechism, no. 1257, emphasis in original).

The will of God is for "all men to be saved and to come to the knowledge of the truth" (1 Tim. 2:4). To fulfill His will, Jesus commissioned the apostles to preach the Gospel and baptize those who would embrace it (cf. Mk. 16:15–16). He gave us the Sacrament of Baptism and unity with the Church as the ordinary means of salvation. By Baptism, we are made sharers in the life of Christ. When we participate in the fullness of life within the Church, we remain obedient children of God, with the Church as our Mother. To provide assurance for the salvation of all men, we must fulfill the command of Christ to evangelize the world and bring all into His Body, the Church.

Because God is not bound by the sacraments, He makes the grace of salvation available to all in ways unknown to us. This is the basis of the Church's teaching on "Baptism of desire" (cf. Catechism, nos. 1258–60, 1281). Baptism of desire occurs, for example, when one seeks Baptism, but dies first, or when one dies without explicit knowledge of Christ, but would have embraced the truth had it been presented. Only God can judge such souls.

The Church is the ark through which men are saved. Noah and his family were the only people saved on the ark, but even animals who had no understanding of the matter were saved with them. As the ark saved all on it, even those who had no knowledge, so does the Church, as the universal sacrament of salvation, dispense the graces won by Christ and apply them to all men of every place and condition. In a way mysterious to us, this salvation is offered to all, and God, Who judges the hearts of all, will determine their destiny.

Salvation Is Found in the Truth

With the coming of the Saviour Jesus Christ, God has willed that the Church founded by him be the instrument for the salvation of *all* humanity (cf. Acts 17:30–31). This truth of faith does not lessen the sincere respect which the Church has for the religions of the world, but at the same time, it rules out, in a radical way, that mentality of indifferentism "characterized by a religious relativism which leads to the belief that 'one religion is as good as another.'" If it is true that the followers of other religions can receive divine grace, it is also certain that *objectively speaking* they are in a gravely deficient situation in comparison with those who, in the Church, have the fullness of the means of salvation. However, "all the children of the Church should nevertheless remember that their exalted condition results, not from their own merits, but from the grace of Christ. If they fail to respond in thought, word, and deed to that grace, not only shall they not be saved, but they shall be more severely judged." One understands then that, following the Lord's command (cf. Mt. 28:19–20) and as a requirement of her love for all people, the Church "proclaims and is in duty bound to proclaim without fail, Christ who is the way, the truth, and the life (Jn. 14:6). In him, in whom God reconciled all things to himself (cf. 2 Cor. 5:18–19), men find the fullness of their religious life."

In inter-religious dialogue as well, the mission *ad gentes* "today as always retains its full force and necessity." "Indeed, God 'desires all men to be saved and come to the knowledge of the truth' (1 Tim. 2:4); that is, God wills the salvation of everyone through the knowledge of the truth. Salvation is found in the truth. Those who obey the promptings of the Spirit of truth are already on the way of salvation. But the Church, to whom this truth has been entrusted, must go out to meet their desire, so as to bring them the truth. Because she believes in God's universal plan of salvation, the Church must be missionary." Inter-religious dialogue, therefore, as part of her evangelizing mission, is just one of the actions of the Church in her mission *ad gentes*. *Equality*, which is a presupposition of inter-religious dialogue, refers to the equal personal dignity of the parties in dialogue, not to doctrinal content, nor even less to the position of Jesus Christ—who is God himself made man—in relation to the founders of the other religions. Indeed, the Church, guided by charity and respect for freedom, must be primarily committed to proclaiming to all people the truth definitively revealed by the Lord, and to announcing the necessity of conversion to Jesus Christ and of adherence to the Church through Baptism and the other sacraments, in order to participate fully in communion with God, the Father, Son and Holy Spirit. Thus, the certainty of the universal salvific will of God does not diminish, but rather increases the duty and urgency of the proclamation of salvation and of conversion to the Lord Jesus Christ.[14]

Questions for Reflection or Group Discussion

1. How would I explain the necessity of the Church to someone who says that all churches are basically equal?

2. The Catholic Church teaches the unicity (oneness) and salvific universality of the mystery of Jesus Christ and His Church, and that the Church of Christ, despite the divisions which exist among Christians, continues to subsist fully only in the Catholic Church. How do I explain such teachings in the face of accusations that they are "unecumenical," "triumphalistic," or "arrogant"?

3. In reaction to rising indifferentism and relativism ("what's right for you isn't necessarily right for me"), some have taken a more rigorous approach to this issue, often identifying with

---

[14] Congregation for the Doctrine of the Faith, Declaration on the Unity and Salvific Universality of Jesus Christ and the Church *Dominus Iesus* (August 6, 2000), no. 22, citations omitted, emphasis in original.

Father Leonard Feeney, who held that those who were not baptized Catholics in a state of grace were necessarily going to hell. This extreme view was condemned by Pope Pius XII in 1949.[15] How do I understand and explain the possibility of salvation beyond the visible boundaries of the Church in a way that doesn't lead to indifferentism or undermine the Church's missionary activity?

---

[15] Cf. F. Cardinal Marchetti-Selvaggiani, "Letter of the Holy Office" (August 8, 1949), in *The Canon Law Digest: Officially Published Documents Affecting the Code of Canon Law* 1942–1953, vol. 3, ed. Rev. T. Lincoln Bouscarren, S.J. (Milwaukee: The Bruce Publishing Company, 1954), 526–30.

Chapter 4

SMELLS, BELLS, AND
OTHER LITURGICAL ODDS AND ENDS
CLEARING UP COMMON MISCONCEPTIONS

Has the Church discouraged or forbidden the use of incense at Mass, the ringing of bells at the Consecration, the use of hand missals and Communion patens, kneeling after receiving Holy Communion, the use of tabernacle veils, or the use of chalice veils?

Almighty God created matter as well as spirit, and the Second Person of the Blessed Trinity sanctified matter by assuming a perfect human nature that included a body as well as a soul. For these reasons, the Church consistently upholds the goodness of matter and opposes those who understand matter as evil or illusory.

In defending the goodness of matter, the Church has always taught that material signs and symbols enrich her liturgical worship. Because matter not only is good but also has been sanctified, sensible things—the things we can see, hear, smell, touch, and taste—can express our worship and draw us closer to God. Almighty God has decreed the use of many particular material signs and symbols in the liturgical worship of the Old and New Testaments.

The Roman Missal, revised in accordance with Vatican II, enshrines this perennial Catholic teaching in current legislation concerning the Holy Sacrifice of the Mass:

> Because . . . the celebration of the Eucharist, like the entire Liturgy, is carried out through perceptible signs that nourish, strengthen, and express faith [*Sacrosanctum Concilium*, no. 59], the utmost care must be taken to choose and to arrange those forms and elements set forth by the Church that, in view of the circumstances of the people and the place, will more effectively

foster active and full participation and more properly respond to the spiritual needs of the faithful. [1]

With the revision of the Roman Missal after Vatican II (1962–65), some formerly mandatory liturgical practices that involve the use of material signs and symbols have become optional; other commonplace practices have fallen into relative disuse. Unfortunately, some have asserted that these practices are now discouraged or forbidden, when in truth they are permitted or even required. While this FAITH FACT does not address all such concerns, the practices discussed below are often mistakenly described as discouraged or forbidden.

Incense at Mass

Incense, mentioned over one hundred times in Sacred Scripture, represents the holiness of God's presence and the prayers of the faithful rising to God. The General Instruction of the Roman Missal (GIRM) teaches, "Thurification or incensation is an expression of reverence and of prayer, as is signified in Sacred Scripture (cf. Ps. 141 [140]: 2; Rev. 8:3)."[2] The Roman Missal of 1962 limited the use of incense to certain Masses. The postconciliar liturgical reform actually *expanded* the use of incense. Indeed, current liturgical legislation permits the use of incense at any Mass.

The GIRM states:

Incense may be used if desired in any form of the Mass:
a. During the Entrance procession;
b. At the beginning of Mass, to incense the cross and the altar;
c. At the Gospel procession and the proclamation of the Gospel itself;
d. After the bread and the chalice have been placed on the altar, to incense the offerings, the cross, and the altar, as well as the priest and people;

---

[1] General Instruction of the Roman Missal (GIRM), 2002 Third Typical Edition (Washington, D.C.: United States Catholic Conference, 2003), no. 20.
[2] GIRM, 2002 ed., no. 276.

e. At the showing of the host and chalice after the consecration.[3]

The GIRM further describes the bows, number of incensations, and other details associated with the use of incense at Mass.[4]

Bells at the Consecration

Bells are mentioned seven times in Sacred Scripture, in every instance in connection with liturgical worship. In six of those seven instances, bells draw attention to the coming of a sacred person.

The Church strongly encourages, but does not require, the ringing of a bell before and after the Consecration in parish and other public churches. In the Mass, the bell indicates the coming of the Person of Jesus Christ and His presence under the appearances of bread and wine at the Consecration:

> A little before the consecration, when appropriate, the server rings a bell as a signal to the faithful. According to local custom, the server also rings the bell as the priest shows the host and the chalice.[5]

In 1972, the following query was put to the Sacred Congregation for Divine Worship and the Discipline of the Sacraments: "Is a bell to be rung at Mass?" The Congregation's authoritative reply follows:

> It all depends on the different circumstances of places and people, as is clear from GIRM, no. 109: "A little before the Consecration, the server may ring a bell as a signal to the faithful. Depending on local custom, he also rings the bell at the showing of both the host and the chalice." From a long

---

[3] GIRM, 2002 ed., no. 276.
[4] Cf. GIRM, 2002 ed., no. 277.
[5] GIRM, 2002 ed., no. 150.

and attentive catechesis and education in liturgy, a particular
liturgical assembly may be able to take part in the Mass with
such attention and awareness that it has no need of this signal
at the central part of the Mass. This may easily be the case, for
example, with religious communities or with particular or
small groups. The opposite may be presumed in a parish or
public church, where there is a different level of liturgical and
religious education, and where often people who are visitors or
are not regular churchgoers take part. In these cases the bell as
a signal is entirely appropriate and is sometimes necessary. To
conclude: usually a signal with the bell should be given, at
least at the two elevations, in order to elicit joy and attention.[6]

Hand Missals

Many of the lay faithful find that hand missals and
missalettes are extraordinarily helpful in fostering their active
participation at Mass. They find that hand missals help them
prepare for Mass by allowing them to meditate upon the
Scripture readings beforehand. They also find that hand missals
prevent their minds from wandering during Mass and allow
them to understand better those who speak with a foreign
accent, or when the acoustics of the church are poor.

The Church has never questioned, let alone legislated
against, the use of hand missals. On the contrary, in 1972, the
following query was put to the Sacred Congregation for Divine
Worship and the Discipline of the Sacraments: "Are hand
missals still needed?" The Congregation replied:

> Since the reform of the liturgy the usefulness of hand missals
> for the faithful is often questioned. All now understand the
> words spoken at Mass; what is more, as far as the biblical read-
> ings are concerned, all ought to be listening attentively to the
> Word of God. Nevertheless, hand missals, it seems, remain
> necessary. People do not always hear well, especially in large
> churches, and what they do hear physically they do not always

---

[6] *Notitiae* 8 (1972), 195–96, as quoted in *Documents on the Liturgy 1963–1979: Conciliar, Papal, and Curial Texts*, trans. Thomas C. O'Brien (Collegeville, Minn.: Liturgical Press, 1982), 494 n. R28.

understand right away. They, therefore, often need to go back over the texts heard during a celebration. In addition, the liturgy, and the Eucharistic celebration above all, is "the summit toward which the activity of the Church is directed; at the same time it is the fount from which all the Church's power flows" (Vatican II, *Sacrosanctum Concilium*, no. 10). All the concerns of the spiritual life must be brought to the liturgy and that happens if participation is truly actual and "aware." This requires frequent meditation on the liturgical texts both before and after the celebration.[7]

The Communion Plate (or Paten)

In Sacred Scripture, being trampled underfoot is a sign of humiliation (cf. Ps. 91:13; Is. 63:3; Mt. 7:6). To prevent the accidental or deliberate profanation of the Blessed Sacrament that would result from Its falling to the ground (and, as it were, being trampled underfoot), the Church requires the use of the communion plate at Mass. The communion plate is a small, flat sacred vessel, usually made of or coated with precious metal, and is held by an altar server under the chin of the communicant during the Communion of the faithful.

The GIRM mandates:

> The following are also to be prepared . . . on the credence table: the chalice, and corporal, a purificator, and, if appropriate a pall; the paten and, if needed, ciboria; bread for the Communion of the priest who presides, the deacon, the ministers, and the people; cruets containing the wine and the water, unless all of these are presented by the faithful in procession at the offertory; the vessel of water to be blessed, if the *asperges* occurs; the Communion-plate for the Communion of the faithful; and whatever is needed for the washing of hands. [8]

There is no provision in the GIRM that dispenses with the use of the communion plate in those nations where, by way of

---

[7] *Notitiae* 8 (1972), 343, as quoted in *Documents on the Liturgy 1963–1979*, 486 n. R18.
[8] GIRM, 2002 ed., no. 118, italics in original.

exception to the norm of the universal Church, Communion in the hand is permitted.

Kneeling before and after Receiving Holy Communion

It is sometimes asserted that kneeling became a sign of adoration only in the High Middle Ages and was never a sign of adoration in biblical times. Such assertions are false. Kneeling is mentioned nearly two dozen times in the Old and New Testaments as a sign of adoration, whether of the one true God or of false gods such as Baal. For this reason, the Church in the United States requires the laity to kneel before receiving Holy Communion, when they adore the God Whom they will receive under the appearances of bread and wine. In addition, the Church permits the laity to kneel after receiving Holy Communion.

In discussing posture, the GIRM states:

> They [the faithful] should . . . sit while the readings before the Gospel and the responsorial Psalm are proclaimed and for the homily and while the Preparation of the Gifts at the Offertory is taking place; and, as circumstances allow, they may sit or kneel while the period of sacred silence after Communion is observed.

> In the dioceses of the United States of America, they should kneel beginning after the singing or recitation of the *Sanctus* until after the *Amen* of the Eucharistic Prayer, except when prevented on occasion by reasons of health, lack of space, the large number of people present, or some other good reason. Those who do not kneel ought to make a profound bow when the priest genuflects after the consecration. The faithful kneel after the *Agnus Dei* unless the Diocesan Bishop determines otherwise.[9]

Tabernacle and Chalice Veils

In descriptions of worship in both the Old and New Testaments, veils separate the sacred from the profane and dis-

---

[9] GIRM, 2002 ed., no. 43, italics in original.

tinguish the varying degrees of the sacred (the holy place and the holy of holies) from each other (cf. Ex. 26; 36; Heb. 6: 19–20; 10:19–20).

According to current liturgical legislation, the tabernacle, in which the Blessed Sacrament is reserved for the Communion of the sick and the worship of adoration, ought to be veiled unless the competent ecclesiastical authority has mandated that a substitution be used. In *Inaestimabile Donum*, the Sacred Congregation for the Sacraments and Divine Worship decreed:

> The presence of the Eucharist is to be indicated by a tabernacle veil or by some other suitable means laid down by the competent authority, and a lamp must perpetually burn before it, as a sign of honor paid to the Lord.[10]

Authority competent to establish other norms includes the Holy See, the bishop in his own diocese, or the conference of bishops with either the unanimous acceptance by all bishop members or the approval of the Holy See.

The Church also advises that the chalice be veiled at Mass until the presentation of the gifts at the offertory. The GIRM states:

> It is a praiseworthy practice to cover the chalice with a veil, which may be either the color of the day or white.[11]

What to Do?

When the practices mentioned above are omitted, it is helpful to make the following distinctions:

—Is the practice an option that is licitly omitted (for example, the use of incense and the ringing of bells at the Consecration), or is it a requirement?

---

[10] Sacred Congregation for the Doctrine of the Faith, Instruction Concerning Worship of the Eucharistic Mystery *Inaestimabile Donum* (April 17, 1980), no. 25.
[11] GIRM, 2002 ed., no. 118.

—Has a false assertion been made (for example, "Vatican II discourages ringing the bells at the Consecration"), or has an action been taken that violates liturgical norms?

—Do charity and prudence dictate that the matter be offered up in silence, or do they dictate that the matter be addressed with the appropriate person(s) candidly, privately, and respectfully?

Many have found CUF's FAITH FACT on liturgical abuse and accompanying protocol helpful in making these distinctions and prudential judgments. This FAITH FACT provides principles that will help determine whether an action contrary to liturgical norms has occurred and how it ought to be addressed. The "Effective Lay Witness Protocol" provides a course of action approved by the Church for addressing such concerns.[12]

The Eucharistic Sacrifice is the source and summit of the life of the Church. May it remain a source of inspiration, unity, and joy for all the faithful.

Questions for Reflection or Group Discussion

1. If my parish priest never uses incense, claiming that "Vatican II did away with that outdated ritual," is he violating the rubrics of the Mass?

2. The purpose of the bells at the Consecration is to direct the attention of the faithful to the coming of Christ under the appearances of bread and wine. Am I usually focused and rec-ollected during the Consecration?

3. Do I tend to be more concerned with how the Mass is being celebrated than with the Mass itself? How can I most effec-tively deal with distractions during the Mass?

---

[12] See "Effective Lay Witness Protocol" in Appendix II.

Chapter 5

A MATTER OF DISTRIBUTION
ORDINARY AND EXTRAORDINARY MINISTERS
OF HOLY COMMUNION

What is an extraordinary minister of Holy Communion? What is the role of lay ministers in the distribution of Holy Communion?

A Eucharistic minister who is not ordained is an extraordinary minister of Holy Communion. The ordinary ministers of Holy Communion are bishops, priests, and deacons, all of whom have received the Sacrament of Holy Orders.

The Church does permit the use of extraordinary ministers of Holy Communion under certain circumstances. The Catechism, quoting the Code of Canon Law [can. 230 § 3], states: "When the necessity of the Church warrants it and when ministers are lacking, lay persons . . . can also . . . distribute Holy Communion in accord with the prescriptions of law" (no. 903).

Supply and Demand

Following the liturgical renewal of Pope Saint Pius X stemming from his decree *Sacra Tridentina Synodus*, there was a great increase in the number of laity who receive Holy Communion regularly.[1] The Church today encourages those who are properly disposed to receive Communion whenever they participate in Mass—even on a daily basis (cf. Catechism, nos. 1388–89). Further, the reception of Communion under both species is more common today, and this practice generally presupposes at least one minister for each species.[2]

---

[1] Cf. Pope Saint Pius X, Decree on Holy Communion *Sacra Tridentina Synodus* (December 20, 1905).

[2] "Since Christ is sacramentally present under each of the species, communion under the species of bread alone makes it possible to receive all the fruit of Eucharistic grace. For pastoral reasons this manner of receiving communion has been legitimately established as the most common form in the Latin rite" (Catechism, no. 1390).

At the same time, in the United States there has been a gradual decrease in the number of ordinary ministers of Holy Communion. For example, in 1962, on the eve of Vatican II, the ratio of priests to laity was 1:771.[3] Based on data from the 2002 *Official Catholic Directory*, the ratio is now 1:1,429, meaning there are now 7 priests per 10,000 Catholics in this country, and the median age of active priests continues to rise.[4] As of 1998, there were 2,460 priestless parishes in the United States.[5]

In light of these developments, the Church today has more frequent recourse to the use of non-ordained or extraordinary ministers for the distribution of Holy Communion. Pope John Paul II has written that "[i]t is obvious that the Church can grant this faculty to those who are neither priests nor deacons."[6] Yet the proliferation of extraordinary ministers of Holy Communion has not been without controversy. On the one hand, there are those who would resist the use of lay ministers of Holy Communion under any circumstances. More frequently, however, the issue is the perceived overuse of extraordinary ministers of Holy Communion, in violation of the Church's guidelines, and the accompanying blurring of the roles of clergy and laity.

Defining Our Terms

It is crucial that we properly understand our terms. As noted above, the ordinary ministers of Holy Communion are bishops, priests, and deacons. Every other minister of Holy Communion is considered extraordinary. "Ordinary" in this sense does not necessarily mean what is customary or usual, but rather "ordained." Similarly, "extraordinary" refers to those who are not ordained. Unfortunately, the term "extraordinary minister"

---

[3] John F. Quinn, "Priest Shortage Panic," *Crisis* (October 1996), 40–44.

[4] *The Official Catholic Directory for the Year of Our Lord 2002* (New Providence, N.J.: P. J. Kennedy & Sons, 2002), 2131, provides that as of 2002, there are 45,713 priests in the United States serving 65,270,444 Catholics.

[5] *The CARA Report*, vol. 4, no. 1 (summer 1998), as cited in U.S. Catholic Bishops, Secretariat for Vocations and Priestly Formation, "Frequently Requested Church Statistics"; available from www.usccb.org/vocations/statistics.htm.

[6] Pope John Paul II, Letter on the Mystery and Worship of the Eucharist *Dominicae Cenae* (February 24, 1980), no. 11.

gives the impression that such ministry must be exercised *rarely* irrespective of the unavailability of ordinary ministers.

Rather, the distinction should be understood this way: An *ordinary* minister is always permitted to distribute Communion, while an *extraordinary* minister may distribute Communion only under certain specified circumstances set forth below. It should be noted, however, that in localities where there is a dire shortage of ordained ministers, such extraordinary circumstances may exist on a relatively long-term basis.

There are two types of extraordinary ministers of Holy Communion: acolytes and other laypersons. The ministry of acolyte, according to canon law, is open to men who have reached a specified age, and there is an installation liturgy at which the candidate receives this non-ordained ministry.[7] In the United States, this ministry is usually reserved to seminarians who are preparing for priesthood. The vast majority of parishes in this country do not have formally installed acolytes.

Other laypersons who are not acolytes can also serve as extraordinary ministers of Holy Communion. The foregoing is summarized in canon 910 of the Code of Canon Law: "The ordinary minister of holy communion is a bishop, presbyter [priest], or deacon. The extraordinary minister of holy communion is an acolyte or another member of the Christian faithful designated according to the norm of can. 230, §3."[8]

Circumstances beyond Our Control

According to a 1973 Vatican instruction, local bishops may permit laypersons to distribute Holy Communion only under the following circumstances:

    a. whenever no priest, deacon, or acolyte is available;
    b. whenever the same ministers are impeded from administering communion because of another pastoral ministry, ill health, or old age;

---

[7] Cf. Pope Paul VI, Motu Proprio *Ministeria Quaedem*, (August 15, 1972), in *Acta Apostolicae Sedis* 64: 529–34, as quoted in *Documents on the Liturgy 1963–1979*, no. 340, 911. The ministry of acolyte in previous times was considered a minor order, but is now called a ministry to clarify that it does not entail the reception of the Sacrament of Holy Orders.

[8] *Code of Canon Law* (Washington, D.C.: Canon Law Society of America, 1983).

    c. whenever the number of faithful wishing to receive com-
munion is so great that the celebration of Mass or the
giving of communion outside Mass would take too long.[9]

    The same Vatican congregation further addressed the matter
in its 1980 instruction concerning worship of the Eucharistic
Mystery.[10] The congregation noted its concern about "frequent
abuses being reported from different parts of the Catholic world,"
including "the confusion of roles, especially regarding the priestly ministry and the role of the laity." One cited example is
"laypeople distributing Communion while the priests refrain
from doing so."[11] After reiterating the above circumstances in
which extraordinary ministers of Holy Communion may be
used, the document goes on to say that "a reprehensible attitude
is shown by those priests who, though present at the celebration, refrain from distributing Communion and leave this task
to the laity."[12]

    These two Church documents also indicate that it is imper-
missible for a lay person to conduct a Communion service when
a priest or deacon is available. The Church has addressed this
subject elsewhere: "The local Ordinary [i.e., bishop] may give
to other extraordinary ministers the faculty to distribute Holy
Communion whenever this seems necessary for the pastoral
good of the faithful, and when no priest, deacon or acolyte is
available."[13]

    Most recently, the 2002 edition of the General Instruction
of the Roman Missal provides:

---

[9] Sacred Congregation of the Sacraments, On Facilitating Reception of Communion
in Certain Circumstances *Immensae Caritatis* (January 29, 1973), no. 1.

[10] Sacred Congregation of the Sacraments, Instruction Concerning Worship of the
Eucharistic Mystery *Inaestimabile Donum* (April 17, 1980).

[11] Sacred Congregation of the Sacraments, *Inaestimabile Donum*, foreword.

[12] Sacred Congregation of the Sacraments, *Inaestimabile Donum*, no. 10.

[13] Sacred Congregation for Divine Worship, On Holy Communion and the Worship
of the Eucharistic Mystery outside of Mass *Eucharistiae Sacramentum* (June 21,
1973), no. 17, as reproduced in Austin Flannery, ed., *Vatican Council II: The
Conciliar and Post-Conciliar Documents*, vol. 1 (Northport, N.Y.: Costello
Publishing, 1998), 246.

The priest may be assisted in the distribution of Communion by other priests who happen to be present. If such priests are not present and there is a very large number of communicants, the priest may call upon extraordinary ministers to assist him, e.g., duly instituted acolytes or even other faithful who have been deputed for this purpose [cf. *Inaestimabile Donum*, no. 10: AAS 72 (1980), 336; *Ecclesiae de mysterio*, art. 8; AAS 89 (1997), 871]. In case of necessity, the priest may depute suitable faithful for this single occasion [cf. Appendix, 1253].

These ministers should not approach the altar before the priest has received Communion, and they are always to receive from the hands of the priest celebrant the vessel containing either species of the Most Holy Eucharist for distribution to the faithful.[14]

Rome Has Spoken

In a 1987 letter to Archbishop John L. May, Apostolic Pro-Nuncio Pio Laghi conveyed the directives of Paul Augustin Cardinal Mayer, head of the Vatican Congregation of Sacraments:

To be sure, the faculty granted to the laity enabling them to distribute Holy Communion as extraordinary ministers of the Eucharist (canons 230 §2; 910 §2) represents without a doubt one of the most suitable forms of lay participation in the Church's liturgical action. On the one hand, this privilege has provided a real help to both the celebrant and to the congregation on occasions when there exists a large number of people receiving Holy Communion. On the other hand, however, in certain instances, significant abuses of this privilege have taken place. Such abuses have led to situations where the *extraordinary* character of this ministry has been lost. At times, it also appears as though the designation of extraordinary ministers becomes a kind of reward to repay those who have worked for the Church.

Cardinal Mayer notes that the abuse he speaks of happens if:

---

[14] General Instruction of the Roman Missal, 2002 ed., no. 162.

—the extraordinary ministers of the Eucharist *ordinarily* distribute Holy Communion together with the celebrant, both when the number of communicants would not require their assistance, and when there are other celebrants present or other ordinary ministers available, though not celebrating; and

—the extraordinary ministers distribute Holy Communion to themselves and to the faithful while the celebrant and concelebrants, if there any, remain inactive.[15]

Also in 1987, the Pontifical Commission for the Authentic Interpretation of the Code of Canon Law, with the approval of Pope John Paul II, officially interpreted relevant Church law as indicating that "when ordinary ministers are present at the Eucharist, whether they are celebrating or not, and are in sufficient number and are not prevented from doing so by other ministries, the extraordinary ministers of the Eucharist are not allowed to distribute Communion to themselves or to the faithful."[16]

More recently, there was the 1997 *Instruction on Certain Questions Regarding the Collaboration of the Non-Ordained Faithful in the Sacred Ministry of Priest*, jointly issued by eight Vatican dicasteries (offices) and approved by the Holy Father. Article 8 of this document reiterates the Church's practice concerning the use of extraordinary ministers of Holy Communion.

The instruction also encourages diocesan bishops to

issue particular norms concerning extraordinary ministers of Holy Communion which, in complete harmony with the universal law of the Church, should regulate the exercise of this function in his diocese. Such norms should provide, amongst other things, for matters such as the instruction in eucharistic doctrine of those chosen to be extraordinary ministers of Holy Communion, the meaning of the service they provide, the

---

[15] Pio Cardinal Laghi, as quoted in *Lay Witness* 9, no. 7 (May 1988): 12.

[16] Pio Cardinal Laghi, *Lay Witness*, 12.

rubrics to be observed, the reverence to be shown for such an august Sacrament and instruction concerning the discipline on admission to Holy Communion.[17]

The instruction also seeks to avoid confusion of clerical and lay roles and calls for the elimination of certain practices, including "extraordinary ministers receiving Holy Communion apart from the other faithful as though concelebrants . . . [and] the habitual use of extraordinary ministers of Holy Communion at Mass thus arbitrarily extending the concept of 'a great number of the faithful.'"[18]

In calling for the elimination of the "habitual use of extraordinary ministers," the instruction does not necessarily intend that the use of extraordinary ministers of Holy Communion be curtailed in all places. Rather, it is saying that they should be used only when such use is truly authorized by the Church. Pastors are not to interpret the criteria in such a way as to make the exceptions be the rule.

The Bishop's Call

In the end, clergy and laity alike are to follow the guidelines of their diocesan bishop in the matter. The Congregation for Divine Worship and the Discipline of the Sacraments recently approved the following norms, which took effect on April 7, 2002:

In practice, the need to avoid obscuring the role of the priest and the deacon as the ordinary ministers of Holy Communion by an excessive use of extraordinary ministers might in some circumstances constitute a reason either for limiting the distribution of Holy Communion under both species or for using intinction instead of distributing the Precious Blood from the chalice.

---

[17] Congregation for the Clergy, Instruction on Certain Questions Regarding the Collaboration of the Non-Ordained Faithful in the Sacred Ministry of Priest, *Ecclesiae de Mysterio* (August 15, 1997), article 8.
[18] Congregation for the Clergy, *Ecclesiae de Mysterio*, article 8.

When the size of the congregation or the incapacity of the bishop, priest, or deacon requires it, the celebrant may be assisted by other bishops, priests, or deacons [cf. GIRM, no. 108]. If such ordinary ministers of Holy Communion are not present, "the priest may call upon extraordinary ministers to assist him, i.e., formally instituted acolytes or even some of the faithful who have been commissioned according to the prescribed rite. In case of necessity, the priest may also commission suitable members of the faithful for the occasion [cf. GIRM, no. 162]." Extraordinary ministers of Holy Communion should receive sufficient spiritual, theological, and practical preparation to fulfill their role with knowledge and reverence. When recourse is had to Extraordinary Minister of Holy Communion, especially in the distribution of Holy Communion under both kinds, their number should not be increased beyond what is required for the orderly and reverent distribution of the Body and Blood of the Lord. In all matters such Extraordinary Ministers of Holy Communion should follow the guidance of the diocesan bishop.[19]

Questions for Reflection or Group Discussion

1. Have I ever served as a minister of Holy Communion? Does my attitude toward extraordinary ministers of Holy Communion reflect the teaching and discipline of the Church?

2. Read Catechism, nos. 1140–44. How do I understand the complementarity of the lay and clerical roles in the sacred liturgy? Why is the Church concerned about keeping these complementary roles distinct from each other?

---

[19] United States Conference of Catholic Bishops, *Norms for the Distribution and Reception of Holy Communion under Both Kinds in the United States of America*, (June 14, 2001), nos. 24, 28; available from http://www.usccb.org/liturgy/current/norms.htm.

Chapter 6

DIVINE EMPOWERMENT
THE SACRAMENT OF CONFIRMATION

What is the Sacrament of Confirmation? How is it significant today?

A sacrament is a physical sign of invisible grace instituted by Jesus Christ as a means of conferring sanctifying grace. Sanctifying grace is the greatest personal encounter with Him in this life, and it prepares us for eternal union with God. *Lumen Gentium*, Vatican II's Dogmatic Constitution on the Church, explains the role of the Sacrament of Confirmation in the spiritual lives of the faithful: "By the sacrament of Confirmation, they are more perfectly bound to the Church and are endowed with the special strength of the Holy Spirit. Hence they are, as true witnesses of Christ, more strictly obliged to spread the faith by word and deed."[1] Confirmation completes baptismal grace by strengthening the individual with the power of the Holy Spirit. It also enlivens the graces of the other sacraments (cf. Catechism, no. 1285). In the Eastern Catholic Churches, Confirmation is known as Chrismation, which refers to the act of anointing with chrism (perfumed oil), which signifies the gift of the Holy Spirit (cf. Catechism, no. 1289).

"Wait for the Promise of the Father"
The scriptural foundations of the Sacrament of Confirmation are largely found in the Acts of the Apostles. However, the Holy Spirit was also at work throughout the Old Testament. God's breath brought about creation (cf. Gen. 1:2). God breathed life into Adam and, therefore, all who are descended

---

[1] Second Vatican Council, Dogmatic Constitution on the Church *Lumen Gentium* (November 21, 1964), no. 11.

from him (cf. Gen. 2:7). God's Spirit rested on the prophets. Joel in particular prophesied the Holy Spirit's arrival at Pentecost (cf. Joel 2:28–29) and was quoted by Peter in his testimony on that day (cf. Acts 2:17–18).

Before Pentecost, Jesus responded to a question about the restoration of the Kingdom of Israel. The apostles were thinking of an earthly kingdom, but Jesus speaks of a heavenly Kingdom: "But you shall receive power when the Holy Spirit has come upon you; and you shall be my witnesses in Jerusalem and in all Judea and Samaria and to the end of the earth" (Acts 1:8). This new power comes from Confirmation. Recall that the Gospels tell of the apostles performing miracles by the power of the Lord. The apostles were already baptized and had faith—however weak—in Jesus. Also, the apostles already knew of the Holy Spirit. They knew that He spoke through the prophets (cf. Acts 1:16) and that He would help them choose an apostle to replace Judas Iscariot (cf. Acts 1:26). This power, to which Jesus refers in Acts 1:8, must have been based on the grace they were already experiencing in their walk with Christ.

The second chapter of Acts tells of the coming of the Holy Spirit on Pentecost, when the apostles become zealous in proclaiming the mighty works of God. Their boldness after receiving the Holy Spirit is sharply contrasted with their weakness and timidity at the arrest of Jesus in the garden of Gethsemane. The apostles then went out and confirmed others, showing Confirmation to be an individual sacrament, distinct from Baptism (cf. Acts 8:14–17; 19:5–6). In addition, the Holy Spirit came down on Jews and Gentiles alike in Caesarea prior to their baptism. Recognizing this as a confirmation by the Holy Spirit, Peter commanded that they be baptized (cf. Acts 10:47).

Sacrament of Power

While Baptism is the sacrament of new life, Confirmation gives birth to that life. Baptism makes us adopted sons of God and brothers of Christ, whereas Confirmation makes us adopted sons in "power" (Acts 1:8) and unites us more fully to the active messianic mission of Christ in the world. Like Baptism, Confirmation places an indelible mark on the soul of the recipient. This character is the seal of the Holy Spirit, Who

clothes the recipient of the sacrament with power to be a witness to Christ (cf. Catechism, no. 1304). Completing baptismal
grace, Confirmation strengthens our bonds of unity with the
Blessed Trinity—with the Father (as His adopted sons), with
the Son (as He has redeemed us), and with the Holy Spirit (as
He gives us His gifts). This sacrament also strengthens our
bonds with the Church, since we all belong to the Family of
God. Confirmation also "gives us a special strength of the Holy
Spirit to spread and defend the faith by word and action as true
witnesses of Christ, to confess the name of Christ boldly, and
never to be ashamed of the Cross [cf. Council of Florence
(1439): DS 1319; LG 11; 12]" (Catechism, no. 1303).

This increase and deepening of baptismal grace through
Confirmation better disposes us to receive the graces of the
other sacraments. Confirmation is the second sacrament of initiation and is traditionally received before First Communion.
As noted by the Sacred Congregation of the Sacraments on
June 30, 1932, "[T]he same Sacred Congregation declared it
was truly opportune and even more conformable to the nature
and effects of the sacrament of confirmation, that children
should not approach the sacred table for the first time unless
after the reception of the sacrament of confirmation, which is,
as it were, the complement of baptism and in which is given
the fullness of the Holy Spirit."[2]

Confirmation strengthens the graces of the other sacraments in various ways. Baptism allows us to participate as
priests, prophets, and kings in Christ's threefold mission.
Confirmation perfects our priestly consecration, anointing us
for an active role in Christian worship, particularly the Holy
Sacrifice of the Mass. In this way, Confirmation is oriented
toward the celebration of the Eucharist (cf. Catechism,
no. 1285). Hence, in the Rite of Christian Initiation for
Adults (RCIA), Confirmation is administered before First
Communion. Further, the spiritual maturity made possible by

---

[2] Sacred Congregation of the Sacraments, *Reply on Age for Confirmation* (June 30,
1932), in *Acta Apostolicae Sedis* 24: 271, as quoted in *The Canon Law Digest*, vol. 1, ed.
T. Lincoln Bouscaren (Milwaukee, Wisc.: The Bruce Publishing Co., 1934), 349.

Confirmation is required for ordination to the priesthood.[3] The Church strongly recommends that couples be confirmed before Marriage;[4] in our age of divorce and family destruction, this sacrament provides graces necessary to help the couple persevere in trials. Also, before administering last rites, a priest can confirm someone who is gravely ill if he has not yet received the sacrament. Finally, the Holy Spirit causes in the confirmed Christian a deepening or intensification of the gifts of wisdom, understanding, and knowledge, which make our minds docile and amenable to what God asks of us. Thus, the penitent is better disposed to receive the graces of the Sacrament of Penance.

Minister, Matter, and Form

In Sacred Scripture, anointing with oil, which signifies the gifts of the Holy Spirit, made someone or something sacred, or set apart for God. In the Bible, kings, prophets, and priests were anointed to carry out their offices. This symbolism is evident in the Sacrament of Confirmation.

"[Bishops] are the original ministers of confirmation."[5] Priests may receive the authority from their bishop to administer this sacrament. In the Eastern Catholic Churches, the priest who baptizes also confirms during the same celebration. However, "he does so with sacred chrism consecrated by the patriarch or the bishop" (Catechism, no. 1312). In the Latin Rite, the priest may confer Confirmation only if the law allows him or if the bishop grants him the necessary faculty to do so (cf. Catechism, no. 1313). Canon law allows Latin Rite priests to confirm under the following circumstances:

1. within the boundaries of their jurisdiction, those who are equivalent in law to a diocesan bishop [i.e.: apostolic administrator or diocesan administrator];

---

[3] Cf. *Code of Canon Law* (Washington, D.C.: Canon Law Society of America, 1983), can. 1033.
[4] Cf. *Code of Canon Law*, can. 1065 §1.
[5] Second Vatican Council, *Lumen Gentium*, no. 26.

2. as regards the person in question, the presbyter [priest] who by virtue of office or mandate of the diocesan bishop baptizes one who is no longer an infant or admits one already baptized into the full communion of the Catholic Church;
3. as regards those who are in danger of death, the pastor or indeed any presbyter [priest].[6]

Anyone who has been baptized may be confirmed. The matter for the Sacrament of Confirmation is chrism (known as myron in the Eastern Catholic Churches) properly consecrated by a bishop. In the Latin Rite, "[t]he matter suitable for a sacrament is olive oil or, according to local conditions, another oil extracted from plants. The chrism is made of oil and some aromatic substance."[7] In the Eastern Catholic Churches, "[The holy myron] is a mixture of olive oil and other herbs and aromatics, sometimes up to forty."[8]

The form of Confirmation is anointing and the laying on of hands. Pope Paul VI provided the Latin Rite with the current formulary in his apostolic constitution on the Sacrament of Confirmation. He decreed: "[T]he sacrament of Confirmation is conferred through the anointing with chrism on the forehead, which is done by the laying on of the hand, and through the words: 'Accipe signaculum doni Spiritus Sancti' [Be sealed with the Gift of the Holy Spirit.] [Paul VI, Divinae consortium naturae, 663]. In the Eastern Churches . . . the more significant parts of the body are anointed with myron: forehead, eyes, nose, ears, lips, chest, back, hands, and feet. Each anointing is accompanied by the formula . . . 'the seal of the gift of the Holy Spirit.' [Rituale per le Chiese orientali di rito bizantino in lingua greca, Pars Prima (Librera Editrice Vaticana, 1954), 36]" (Catechism, no. 1300).

---

[6] Code of Canon Law, can. 883.
[7] Rite for the Blessing of Oils and Rite of Consecrating the Chrism, nos. 3–4, as quoted in William Woestman, Sacraments: Initiation, Penance, Anointing of the Sick (Ottawa: St. Paul University, 1992), 76.
[8] Victor J. Pospishil, Eastern Catholic Church Law (New York: St. Maron Publications, 1996), 392, citation omitted.

Not Just for Grown-Ups

In the early Church, the order of receiving the sacraments of initiation was Baptism, Confirmation, and Holy Eucharist. As various documents of local councils attest, the accepted age of Confirmation in the Latin Rite traditionally was the age of reason, which is presumed at age seven (cf. Catechism, no. 1307). Despite this well-documented and ancient practice, by the turn of the twentieth century it was common for children to receive Confirmation and First Communion after the age of ten, at times in the same celebration. When Pope Saint Pius X lowered the age of First Communion to the age of reason, most dioceses did not lower the age of Confirmation. As a result, in most Latin Rite dioceses of the United States, Confirmation was deferred until after First Communion, usually until a person is in the teenage years. Although Confirmation has become known as the sacrament of Christian maturity, it is not restricted to young adults:

> Although Confirmation is sometimes called the "sacrament of Christian maturity," we must not confuse adult faith with the adult age of natural growth, nor forget that the baptismal grace is a grace of free, unmerited election and does not need "ratification" to become effective. St. Thomas reminds us of this:
>
>> Age of body does not determine age of soul. Even in childhood man can attain spiritual maturity: as the book of *Wisdom* says: "For old age is not honored for length of time, or measured by number of years." Many children, through the strength of the Holy Spirit they have received, have bravely fought for Christ even to the shedding of their blood [St. Thomas Aquinas *STh* III, 72, 8, *ad* 2; cf. Wis. 4:8] (Catechism, no. 1308).

Current Church discipline in the United States allows for both practices. "Following recognition by the Holy See, the United States Conference of Catholic Bishops has decreed that the age for conferring the sacrament of Confirmation in the

Latin Rite dioceses of the United States will be between 'the age of discretion and about sixteen years of age.'"[9]

Questions for Reflection
or Group Discussion

1. In past decades, Confirmation was described as making us "soldiers for Christ." Today we often hear of Confirmation as being the sacrament of "Christian maturity." How do I understand this sacrament? What is the mind of the Church in this regard? (See Catechism, no. 1316.)

2. What advantages are there in celebrating the Sacrament of Confirmation once the child attains the age of reason, rather than waiting for the teen years?

3. Am I aware of the Holy Spirit's action in my life? Does my life manifest the fruits of the Spirit? How can I become more docile to the promptings of the Holy Spirit?

---

[9] United States Conference of Catholic Bishops, Office of Communications, "Age of Confirmation Decreed" (November 10, 2002); available from http://www.usccb.org/comm/archives/2001/01-150.htm.

Morality Is Habit-Forming
The Cardinal Virtues

What are the cardinal virtues? What is the role of the cardinal virtues in the Christian life?

"A virtue is a habitual and firm disposition to do the good" (Catechism, no. 1803). The two types of virtues mentioned in the Catechism are *theological* and *human* (or *moral*) virtues. The theological virtues of faith, hope, and charity "relate directly to God" (Catechism, no. 1812), are given to us at Baptism, and allow us to live a life of supernatural grace as children of God (cf. Catechism, nos. 1812–13).

The immediate object of the human virtues is not God, but human activities that lead us to God. They are generally acquired by human effort, but are assisted and reach their perfection by grace. These virtues help us to lead a morally good life with joy and relative ease (cf. Catechism, no. 1804).

There are four human (or moral) virtues known as *cardinal* virtues. "Cardinal" comes from the Latin word *cardo*, which means "hinge." The cardinal virtues, then, are considered the "hinge virtues" and are the basis of all the other human virtues. The cardinal virtues are prudence, justice, fortitude, and temperance.

Sacred Scripture frequently attests to the value of these virtues in living a godly life, although sometimes they are called by other names. For example, the author of the Book of Wisdom teaches, "And if any one loves righteousness, [wisdom's] labors are virtues; for she teaches self-control [that is, temperance] and prudence, justice and courage [that is, fortitude]; nothing in life is more profitable for men than these" (Wis. 8:7).

Character Building 101

The Catechism defines the cardinal virtues as "stable disposi-tions of the intellect and the will that govern our acts, order our passions, and guide our conduct in accordance with reason and faith" (no. 1834). They help us to make good moral choices and thus are an indispensable part of the Christian life.

The moral virtues—like all habits—are acquired and "grow through education, deliberate acts, and perseverance in strug-gle" (Catechism, no. 1839). They can be diminished or lost by the repetition of acts that are opposed to the virtue. These acts not only destroy the virtue, but typically replace it with the opposite vice. When, in addition, we fail to practice a partic-ular virtue, it will gradually weaken and die.

We need to recognize that because of original sin, our human nature is wounded and prone to sin and vice. Our new life in Christ gives us the grace to persevere in virtuous living. As a result, we "should always ask for this grace of light and strength, frequent the sacraments, cooperate with the Holy Spirit, and follow his calls to love what is good and shun evil" (Catechism, no. 1811). We need to be humble enough to recognize our sinful tendencies and to cultivate the opposite virtues. In this way, we build a character worthy of our calling.

As we grow in virtue, it becomes easier for us to recognize the true and choose the good, and thus we experience the freedom of the children of God (cf. Jn. 8:32; Gal. 5:1). When we choose evil, we abuse our freedom and fall prey "to the slavery of sin" (cf. Catechism, no. 1733). Saint Paul says, "[W]hatever is true, whatever is honorable, whatever is just, whatever is pure, what-ever is lovely, whatever is gracious, if there is any excellence, if there is anything worthy of praise, think about these things" (Phil. 4:8).

Prudence

Prudence is the cardinal virtue that "disposes the practical reason to discern, in every circumstance, our true good and to choose the right means for achieving it" (Catechism, no. 1835). With the help of prudence, we learn from our experiences and correctly bring moral principles to bear upon real-life situations (cf. Catechism, no. 1806). Saint Thomas Aquinas emphasizes that prudence enables us to choose good means to a good end. It guides our practical decision-making in individual, concrete circumstances and provides for effective execution once a decision is reached.[1]

The three stages of prudence are deliberation, judgment, and decision. Note that hesitation is appropriate when it comes to deliberation: One can and should consider all the facts and moral principles that bear upon the situation and be open to human and divine counsel. Once a decision has been made, it should be performed swiftly. For example, if a person in authority asks us to do something that may be inappropriate, we should consider whether it would be prudent to obey. If we discern, however, that such a request constitutes a legitimate exercise of authority, our decision to obey should be promptly acted upon.

Errors in judgment can creep in through defects of prudence or through "false prudence." Defects include thoughtlessness, rashness, negligence, indecisiveness, and inconstancy in execution. False prudence takes two forms. One is the giving in to the "prudence of the flesh," thus making decisions based solely on serving the goods of the body, which Saint Paul criticizes as being displeasing to God and leading to death (cf. Rom. 8:6–8). The other form is what Saint Thomas calls *astutia*, which is often translated as "cunning" or "craftiness." *Astutia* is concerned more with "tactics" than living in the light. True prudence is concerned not only with a good end, but also with good means to that end. On the other hand, *astutia* is the insidious temperament of the intriguer who will use any means to obtain the desired end.

Prudence is often called the first of the cardinal virtues. As the "charioteer of the virtues" (Catechism, no. 1806), it guides the other virtues and guides the judgment of conscience. Indeed, there is no way we can have a well-formed conscience without the virtue of prudence (cf. Catechism, nos. 1780, 1788).

In the Book of Tobit, we are advised to "[s]eek advice from every wise man, and do not despise any useful counsel. Bless the Lord God on every occasion; ask him that your ways may be

---

[1] Cf. Saint Thomas Aquinas, *Summa Theologiae*, IIa IIae, q. 47, art. 6; available from http://www.newadvent.org/summa/304706.htm.

made straight and that all your paths and plans may prosper"
(Tob. 4:18–19). This passage encourages us to learn and take
counsel from others in true humility and docility. It also encourages us to seek the Lord's assistance. Through counsel, one of
the gifts of the Holy Spirit (cf. Is. 11:1–2), prudence is purified
and directed toward our ultimate good, God Himself.

Justice

"Justice consists in the firm and constant will to give God
and neighbor their due" (Catechism, no. 1836). Justice in
relation to God is called the virtue of religion. Justice toward
our neighbor disposes us to respect the rights of others, and to
foster harmony in human relationships rooted in the truth
(cf. Catechism, no. 1807).

Duty is the debt of justice we owe to others. With every duty
is a corresponding right. If I have a duty to pay a ten dollar debt,
for example, my creditor has a right to receive it. Rights can
arise in a variety of social, economic, or political contexts.
There are some fundamental rights, however, that preexist
human laws or business transactions. These are rights given to
us by God, that we have by virtue of our being created in His
image and likeness (cf. Gen. 1:26). These include the right to
life, the right to religious liberty, and the right to earn an honest
living. When individuals or governments fail to recognize these
rights, they act contrary to the truth of creation. In other words,
they act unjustly.

Psalm 112 calls the just man a "light . . . in the darkness" (Ps.
112:4). Conversely, when we succumb to injustice, and "call evil
good and good evil" (Is. 5:20), we are "already on the path to the
most alarming corruption and the darkest moral blindness."[2]

There are three basic forms of justice (cf. Catechism, no.
2411). *Commutative* justice is the justice that individuals owe
one another. *Distributive* justice describes the relation of the
whole to its parts. Specifically, it describes the duties the government owes its citizens, including the protection of their
fundamental rights. *Legal* justice describes the relation of the

---

[2] Pope John Paul II, Encyclical Letter on the Value and Inviolability of Human Life
Evangelium Vitae (March 25, 1995), no. 24.

citizens to the state—for example, the obligation to "[r]ender to Caesar the things that are Caesar's" (Mk. 12:17), such as the payment of taxes.

Also included under justice is the Church's social teaching, which often comes under the general heading of "social justice." The social doctrine of the Church has seen remarkable development since the nineteenth century. The most important Church documents on this subject over the past century include: *Rerum Novarum, Quadragesimo Anno, Gaudium et Spes, Populorum Progressio, Laborem Exercens, Sollicitudo Rei Socialis, Centesimus Annos.* This body of teaching provides principles about social and economic matters that involve the promotion of fundamental human rights and the common good (see Catechism, nos. 2419–42).

Fortitude

Fortitude is the cardinal virtue that ensures a steadiness of the will in the pursuit of the good notwithstanding any difficulties (cf. Catechism, no. 1808). This virtue allows us to maintain our balance in the face of danger. On the one extreme, we need to avoid cowardice, which involves giving in to the passion of fear. On the other, we must avoid rashness or recklessness, which involves imprudently subjecting ourselves to temptation or some physical danger.

The virtue of fortitude has two facets: to attack and to endure. Of the two, fortitude more fully shows itself in patient endurance—when there is no reasonable hope of conquering the evil that is threatening us. Patience, however, is much more than mere submission to danger and suffering. Rather, it is a strong quality of the soul that allows us to cling steadfastly to the good and refuse to yield to fear or pain.

Ultimately, the virtue of fortitude enables us to conquer even the fear of death, and thus face trials and persecutions willingly and even joyfully (cf. Catechism, no. 1808). For the Christian, the supreme act of fortitude is martyrdom: "*Martyrdom* is the supreme witness given to the truth of the faith: it means bearing witness even unto death. The martyr bears witness to Christ who died and rose, to whom he is united by charity. He bears witness to the truth of the faith and of Christian doctrine. He

endures death through an act of fortitude" (Catechism, no.
2473, emphasis in original). In Revelation 12:10–11, those who
have conquered the powers of evil are those who "loved not
their lives even unto death."

Yet this willingness to fall in battle must be understood
properly. Fortitude is not authentic unless it is grounded in
prudence and justice. It is completely opposed to a reckless or
daredevil approach to danger. The truly virtuous man does not
suffer injury or martyrdom for its own sake, but as a means to
preserve or acquire a greater good. The Gospel summarizes this
paradox: "He who loves his life loses it, and he who hates his life
in this world will keep it for eternal life" (Jn. 12:25).

Temperance

The Catechism defines temperance as "the moral virtue that
moderates the attraction of pleasures and provides balance in
the use of created goods. It ensures the will's mastery over
instincts and keeps desires within the limits of what is honorable" (no. 1809). Temperance helps us "to live sober, upright,
and godly lives in this world" (Tit. 2:12).

While fortitude is self-possession in a sea of danger, temperance is self-possession during a storm of passion. Too often,
temperance is equated with a puritanical approach to creation and legitimate human pleasures, in effect being limited to
avoiding excessive pleasure. In reality, temperance is a positive
ordering of our bodily appetites for our own good and the good
of society. Temperance allows us to be fully ourselves and not
slaves to food, alcohol, sex, gambling, comfort, success, or other
pleasures that may result from excessive indulgence in them
(cf. Catechism, no. 2290). Although this inner ordering of the
bodily appetites produces what Saint Thomas Aquinas calls a
"tranquility of soul,"[3] it requires vigilance, discipline, and
grace because of our fallen human nature.

The surest way to walk a straight line in the snow is to keep
our eyes focused on our destination. We may be tempted to look

---

[3] Saint Thomas Aquinas, *Summa Theologiae*, IIa IIae, q. 141, art. 2, rep. obj. 2; available from http://www.newadvent.org/summa/314102.htm.

at our feet and simply put one in front of the other, but eventually we'll drift off (if we don't first walk into a tree!). This points to the importance of *humility*, which helps us to see ourselves as we truly are: creatures who are at once both sinful and redeemed. More fundamentally, humility orients us toward God, Who is both our origin and our goal. This virtue is no less than temperance as it relates to our quest for excellence, which for the Christian is to "attain to . . . the stature of the fullness of Christ" (Eph. 4:13).

The Family of Moral Virtues

All the moral virtues are in some way related to one of the cardinal virtues. Here are some examples:

Prudence—making good decisions
- *Good counsel* profits from the advice of others when confronted with difficult decisions.
- *Common sense* is the ability to judge things according to the ordinary rules of conduct.
- *Good judgment* involves attentiveness to the mind of the lawmaker.
- *Innocence* helps us to see the truth clearly (cf. 2 Cor. 11:3).
- *Docility* is the ability to be taught.

Justice—giving others their due
- *Religion* is the worship we owe to God.
- *Piety* is the duty that we owe to our parents (and by extension to clergy, our spiritual fathers, and to our family) and to our country, or "fatherland."
- *Observance* refers to the respect owed to those persons distinguished by their office or some dignity.
- *Obedience* is the duty owed to those in authority.
- *Truthfulness* ensures that our communications reflect objective reality.

- *Gratitude* is the duty owed to one who has conferred benefits on us.
- *Zeal* involves eagerly leading others to the good or protecting them from evil.
- *Restitution* is the making of reparation for harm done to others.

Fortitude—constancy in the pursuit of the good

- *Magnanimity* is literally "the quality of being great souled" and inclines us to heroic acts of virtue.
- *Magnificence* leads us to do great things at great personal expense.
- *Patience* enables us to remain at peace despite trials and opposition.
- *Perseverance* helps us to pursue a good cause to the end and reaches its perfection in the distinctly Christian virtue of *martyrdom*.

Temperance—moderation in all things

- *Clemency* remits or lessens the punishment due to a guilty person.
- *Meekness* is self-possession in the face of adversity and thus is even able to restrain justified anger.
- *Modesty* allows us to be self-assured without being self-absorbed or calling undue attention to ourselves. It involves moderation in our dress, language, and behavior.
- *Abstinence* is moderation in the consumption of food for our spiritual welfare.
- *Sobriety* is the regulation of our consumption of food—and especially alcohol and medicines—according to the dictates of reason.
- *Diligence* regulates our desire for ease and comfort.
- *Chastity* controls our desire for sexual pleasure in conformity with reason and the teachings of Christ (cf. Catechism, nos. 2337–91).

Questions for Reflection
or Group Discussion

1. What images come to mind when I hear the words *prudence* and *temperance*? How do these images compare with the true meaning of these terms?

2. See the virtues related to justice on pages 57–58. Do I give others what is due to them out of justice? Read Luke 6:37–38. Do I show understanding toward those who owe me a debt?

3. Gluttony, drunkenness, and lust are cited throughout Scripture as serious sins (cf. 1 Corinthians 6:9–10). What can I do to foster the virtues of sobriety and chastity in my own life and in the lives of others?

Chapter 8

FOLLOWING OUR BISHOPS
APOSTOLIC AUTHORITY IN THE CHURCH

As a Catholic, I understand that the pope has authority over the entire Church. What, then, is the role of my local bishop? What should my attitude be toward him?

In the Catechism, the Church teaches that "[t]he faithful . . . should be closely attached to the bishop as the Church is to Jesus Christ, and as Jesus Christ is to the Father [LG 27 § 2]" (no. 896, omission in original). In communion with the whole Church, and under the guidance of the pope, bishops are called to exercise authority in the name of Christ in their respective dioceses. Because the bishop is truly a successor of the apostles, our attitude should be characterized by charity, respect, and obedience.

Divine Institution
While the Family of God in the Old Testament was built on the twelve sons of Israel, the Kingdom of God in the New Testament is built on the firm foundation of the Twelve Apostles. In selecting these apostles, Christ brought them together in a "permanent assembly" (Catechism, no. 880). At the head of this single apostolic assembly, or college, Christ placed Peter, who was chosen from among the Twelve (cf. Catechism, no. 880).

"This pastoral office of Peter and the other apostles belongs to the Church's very foundation and is continued by the bishops under the primacy of the Pope" (Catechism, no. 881). Vatican II affirms that "bishops by divine institution have succeeded to the place of the apostles, as shepherds of the Church, and he who hears them, hears Christ, and he who rejects them, rejects Christ and Him who sent Christ."[1]

---

[1] Second Vatican Council, Dogmatic Constitution on the Church *Lumen Gentium* (November 21, 1964), no. 20.

In a lawless age that disrespects the authority of God—the Source of all authority—it is not surprising that the authority of bishops as successors of the apostles is not respected today. It is thus more important than ever that we understand and manifest in our words and actions the respect due to the sacred authority that our Lord has entrusted to our shepherds.

On the Same Team

It is important to understand that our bishop is neither a mere representative of the pope nor an authority apart from the pope. He exercises authority in the name of Christ in his diocese in communion with the entire Church (cf. Catechism, no. 895).

Catholics are obliged to remain staunchly loyal to all bishops who are in communion with the pope, particularly to one's own bishop. It is not the layperson's role (nor even within the layperson's authority) to judge whether a bishop is in communion with the pope. Rather, only the pope makes this decision. We cannot drive a wedge between the universal Church, represented by the pope, and the diocesan (or particular) Church, headed by the bishop. There are only two possibilities: Either we're in communion with the pope *and* his bishops, or we're not.

In an address given on November 20, 1999 (quoting extensively from the Second Vatican Council's *Lumen Gentium*), Pope John Paul II gave the following teaching on how the laity should relate to their bishops, and derivatively to their priests:

> I likewise point out the attitude that the laity should have towards their Bishops and priests: "To their Pastors they should disclose their needs and desires with that liberty and confidence which befits children of God and brothers of Christ. . . . If the occasion arises, this should be done through the institutions established by the Church for that purpose and always with truth, courage and prudence and with reverence and charity towards those who, by reason of their office, represent the person of Christ."
>
> Unity with the Bishop is the essential and indispensable attitude of the faithful Catholic, for one cannot claim to be on the

Pope's side without also standing by the Bishops in communion with him.

Nor can one claim to be with the Bishops without standing by the Head of the College.[2]

All those who have been reborn in Christ through baptism are called to cooperate in the building up of the Body of Christ (cf. Catechism, nos. 871–73). A proper understanding of the complementarity of roles in the Church, particularly the relationship of the lay faithful with their pastors, is especially important today as the laity strive to take their rightful place in the life of the Church and the "new evangelization." Vatican II stressed the laity's baptismal dignity and consequent call to holiness and mission. The clericalism that may have characterized past generations, whereby the faithful are encouraged to "leave everything to Father," must be rejected.

Conversely, an active, evangelizing laity cannot fail to maintain communion of mind and heart with the local Church. God saves us as a people, as a family, and not as isolated individuals.[3] Accordingly, the laity's approach to the apostolate must be that of collaborators, not "lone rangers." On this point, the Catechism quotes Saint Ignatius of Antioch, a disciple of Saint John the Apostle: "Let no one do anything concerning the Church in separation from the bishop [*Ad Smyrn.* 8, 1: *Apostolic Fathers*, II/2, 309]" (no. 896).

Visible Sources of Unity

Unity is an attribute of God; He is one. Christ is one with His Father and fervently prayed that His disciples would fully experience that unity (cf. Jn. 17:20–21). Unity in the family, in the Church, and in all social structures is a reflection of God's unity; the disunity we encounter reminds us of the lingering effects of sin in our lives and in the world. Unity requires obedience to lawful authority, and all such authority is derived from God. Those to whom God has entrusted authority should exercise such authority for the sake of unity.

---

[2] Pope John Paul II, Address of the Holy Father to the German Bishops on the Occasion of Their "Ad Limina" Visit (November 20, 1999), no. 7.
[3] Cf. Second Vatican Council, *Lumen Gentium*, no. 9.

Vatican II emphasizes that "individual bishops . . . are the visible principle and foundation of unity in their particular churches."[4] How do bishops exercise their authority in the service of unity?

The Church teaches that there are visible bonds of unity in the Church:

—profession of one faith received from the Apostles;
—common celebration of divine worship, especially of the sacraments;
—apostolic succession through the sacrament of Holy Orders, maintaining the fraternal concord of God's family [cf. UR 2; LG 14; CIC, can. 205] (Catechism, no. 815).

These three elements—profession of faith, sacraments, and Church governance—are directly related to the threefold mission of the bishop to teach, sanctify, and rule, which in turn relates to the threefold ministry of Christ as prophet, priest, and king.

The bishop's primary task is to teach, to fulfill the Lord's commandment to preach the Gospel to the whole world. An individual bishop—excluding the pope—does not possess the charism of infallibility, but as a successor of the apostles he nonetheless is an authentic teacher of the Christian faith "endowed with the authority of Christ [LG 25]" (Catechism, no. 888).

The bishop's role is also priestly, and so he is called to offer sacrifice on behalf of the people. As a high priest of the New Covenant, this does not involve offering lambs and calves, but rather the Body and Blood of Jesus Christ, the eternal High Priest, through his sacramental ministry. Accordingly, the Eucharist is the center of the life of each diocese, and the bishop is an agent of salvation, through whom Christ nourishes His flock (cf. Catechism, no. 893).

The bishop is also vested with the authority and sacred power to govern the particular Church entrusted to him. This authority is not given as a means of lording it over the faithful

---

[4] Second Vatican Council, *Lumen Gentium*, no. 23.

entrusted to him (cf. Mt. 20:25–28). Rather, this fatherly authority is exercised in a spirit of service and pastoral charity. The
bishop's role is to foster ecclesial communion, gathering diverse
people with diverse talents and gifts into one Eucharistic
assembly, from which he commissions them to transform the
world. As Cardinal George writes, "Like and in God the Son,
the bishop as servant gathers the baptized into the Eucharistic
assembly and sends them on mission to transform the
world."[5] In this way, he washes the feet of the faithful entrusted to him (cf. Jn. 13:1–17), and strengthens the unity of the
Catholic Church.

Building Family Ties

James Cardinal Hickey affirmed in 1996 that our "true common ground" as Catholics "is found in Scripture and Tradition
as handed on through the teaching office of the Holy Father
and the bishops. Indeed, we are fortunate to have a reliable and
complete expression of our 'common ground' in the *Catechism
of the Catholic Church*."[6]

On occasion, we may have reason to believe that a bishop
or one of his representatives is straying from this common
ground. It is then our role as laity to engage in dialogue—charitably, respectfully, and privately—to build Catholic unity with
the individuals involved. How do we do this? Three rock-solid
principles always apply.

First, the Gospel commands us to love everyone, even
when this love involves personal suffering and sacrifice (cf.
Mt. 5:43–48; Jn. 15:12–27). Vatican II's document on the
apostolate of lay people reminds us that charity, drawn from
the Eucharist above all, "is the soul of the entire apostolate."[7]
Without charity we can do nothing (cf. 1 Cor. 13:1–3), except
make matters worse, and as Vatican II teaches us, "He is not

---

[5] Francis Cardinal George, O.M.I., "Authority, Service, and Communion," in *Servants
of the Gospel* (Steubenville, Ohio: Emmaus Road, 2000), 35.
[6] James Cardinal Hickey, "Catholic Common Ground," *Lay Witness* 17, no. 8 (October
1996): 17.
[7] Second Vatican Council, Decree on the Apostolate of the Laity *Apostolicam
Actuositatem* (November 18, 1965), no. 3.

saved . . . who . . . does not persevere in charity."[8] We should pray regularly and fervently for those in authority (cf. 1 Tim. 2:1–4), and even if a particularly difficult matter is not resolved to our satisfaction, as long as charity has permeated our actions, our Lord will say to us, "Well done, good and faithful servant" (Mt. 25:21).

Second, since bishops are our spiritual fathers, we are commanded to honor them as such by the Fourth Commandment. The *Catechism of the Council of Trent*, citing Matthew 23:2–3, teaches, "Christ the Lord commands obedience even to wicked pastors."[9]

Third, since bishops have lawful authority from Christ Himself, we owe obedience to lawful exercises of such authority, as is true with any legitimate earthly authority.

CUF founder H. Lyman Stebbins used a biblical example to describe our actions if we feel our bishop is in error. Shortly after the great flood, Noah became drunk. The noble patriarch was undeniably wrong in his actions, but his faithful sons walked in backwards and covered their father's nakedness (cf. Gen. 9:23). They proved their loyalty and received their father's blessing. Should difficulties arise, we too must prove our loyalty (and not just our orthodoxy) if we desire our heavenly Father's blessing. We prove this loyalty by using the procedures established by the Church for addressing difficulties. In this way, we remain faithful to the Church, and respectful of the role of the bishop.[10]

Bishops are human beings and consequently are not exempt from the frailties and weaknesses all of us experience in this life. The conduct or teaching of these human vessels may not always be worthy of an apostle of Jesus Christ, just as the conduct of many laity is not always worthy of a disciple of Jesus Christ. Yet Catholics should manifest a filial or childlike piety in all our dealings with bishops and priests by virtue of

---

[8] Second Vatican Council, *Lumen Gentium*, no. 14.
[9] John A. McHugh and Charles J. Callan, trans., *Catechism of the Council of Trent* (South Bend, Ind.: Marian Publications, 1972), 415.
[10] See "Effective Lay Witness Protocol" in Appendix II.

their office as our spiritual fathers. With patience, fortitude, and charity, we always must preserve unity in our pursuit of Christ's truth.

Questions for Reflection or Group Discussion

1. Do I realize that my bishop is a successor of the apostles and is endowed with the authority of Christ, even if he is not infallible? How should this realization affect my attitude toward my bishop?

2. The visible bonds of unity in the Church are the creed, the sacraments, and the Church's governance (cf. Catechism, no. 815). How do these bonds of unity relate to the ministry of the bishop?

3. What practical things can I do to manifest my loyalty and fidelity to my bishop?

Chapter 9

ON EARTH AS IT IS IN HEAVEN
THE NECESSITY OF LAW AND RIGHT ORDER

What is the purpose of law and order?

"In the beginning God created the heavens and the earth. The earth was without form and void, and darkness was upon the face of the deep; and the Spirit of God was moving over the face of the waters. . . . The LORD God took the man and put him in the garden of Eden to till it and keep it. And the LORD God commanded the man, saying, 'You may freely eat of every tree of the garden; but of the tree of the knowledge of good and evil you shall not eat, for in the day that you eat of it you shall die'" (Gen. 1:1–2; 2:15–17).

These passages are familiar to anyone raised within a Christian tradition. In fact, they are also an integral part of Judaism. Yet while these passages are familiar, we may not have fully mined the wisdom within them. They provide a fundamental understanding of the necessity of law and order within any society, including the Church.

Law and order express the presence and will of God. In the absence of law and order, chaos exists. Obedience to lawful authority is an ordinary means of working out our salvation.

The Ordinance of Reason

Divine law is given by God, and human law is given by man (cf. Catechism, no. 1952). Divine law can be eternal, natural, or positive. Human law can be ecclesiastical or secular.

Because the use of reason demands order, law is a necessary consequence of the use of reason. Being reasonable protects truth and results in right order; being unreasonable denies truth and results in chaos. Stated another way, law flows from practical reason. "All law finds its first and ultimate truth in the eternal law" (Catechism, no. 1951), through which God governs the entire universe. The natural law is our participation as creatures in God's wisdom and goodness: "The natural law, present in the heart of each man and established by reason, is universal in its precepts and its authority extends to all men. It expresses the dignity of the person and determines the basis for his fundamental rights and duties" (Catechism, no. 1956). The natural law within each person moves us to grace and inclines us to salvation. Divine positive law—for example, the Ten Commandments—is the law expressly revealed by God. All divine law, both natural and revealed, finds its perfection in the Gospel of Jesus Christ (cf. Catechism, no. 1965).

Human law, both ecclesiastical and secular, should likewise reflect our participation in divine law. We are created in the image and likeness of God. Because law and order reflect the perfect nature of God, and order is intrinsic to the nature of God, man naturally desires order. We are social creatures. Human laws are not eternal or infallible, but they are necessary for right order in society. Insofar as they respect divine law in its various forms and expressions, human laws are good and protect truth. They protect us from sin and guide us to heaven's glory. Insofar as they do not respect divine law, they tend toward chaos and evil and do not protect right order. They lead to death. By necessity, as we grow in our understanding of divine law, and as situations change, human laws require reform and change.

Saint Paul taught that human law ultimately comes from God: "Let every person be subject to the governing authorities. For there is no authority except from God, and those that exist have been instituted by God. Therefore he who resists the authorities resists what God has appointed, and those who resist will incur judgment" (Rom. 13:1–2).

The existence of right order bears witness to the orderly creative work and presence of God, Who created the world in right order and gave it laws to govern its existence (cf. Gen. 1–2:4), and created man to govern the earth (cf. Gen. 1:26–28). Because man rules over the created order, the created order is subject to the blessings and curses of man. Saint Paul teaches:

"For the creation waits with eager longing for the revealing of the sons of God; for the creation was subjected to futility, not of its own will but by the will of him who subjected it in hope; because the creation itself will be set free from its bondage to decay and obtain the glorious liberty of the children of God" (Rom. 8:19–21).

For Our Own Good

In Genesis 2:15–25, two critical points concerning law and right order are revealed. First, law in itself is not a result of sin. It is intrinsic to our nature. Even before sin, even before God completed the creation of man with the creation of woman, He demanded obedience or death from Adam. If Adam freely chose obedience to God, he would share in the fullness of revelation and glory. If he chose disobedience to the direct command from God, he would die. Second, laws must be passed from the one in authority to those subject to authority. God gave Adam the order not to eat from the tree of knowledge of good and evil (cf. Gen. 2:17). Eve apparently knew of this command (cf. Gen. 3:3).

In the same way, God has given us revealed truth and granted lawful authority to the successors of the apostles. They are bound both to teach and to expound the revealed truths for the right order of society. They fulfill these obligations by their word, by their example, and by promulgating ecclesiastical laws that protect justice.

When Satan tempted Eve, he did so by attacking the one command God had given Adam. In the breaking of this command, sin and suffering entered the world (cf. Gen. 3). So began salvation history. This episode reveals two other principles concerning law and authority. First, authority is given to guide and protect others. Conversely, when human laws no longer guide and protect, when they no longer assist us to achieve our true good, they no longer bind. God gave Adam one command to protect his innocence and guide his freedom with responsible obedience. Adam was obligated to pass this on to Eve to protect her from sin.

Second, when one in authority disobeys, all under his authority suffer. The disobedience of Eve did not result in a curse to all men until Adam's disobedience. Her disobedience drew him to sin, but his disobedience resulted in the futility suffered by creation even to this present day (cf. Rom. 5:12–14; 8:20). Adam chose to sin and, as God promised, the consequence was death for him and for all others.

Spirit of Love and Service

Love is the fulfillment of all law: "Teacher, which is the great commandment in the law? And he said to him, 'You shall love the Lord your God with all your heart, and with all your soul, and with all your mind. This is the great and the first commandment. And a second is like it, You shall love your neighbor as yourself. On these two commandments depend all the law and the prophets'" (Mt. 22:36–40).

Recognizing this truth, Saint Paul wrote: "Would you have no fear of him who is in authority? Then do what is good, and you will receive his approval, for he is God's servant for your good. . . . Owe no one anything, except to love one another; for he who loves his neighbor has fulfilled the law" (Rom. 13:3–4, 8).

Saint Paul reminds us in his Letter to the Galatians that those who are guided by the Spirit have crucified their passions and live not for themselves, but for the glory of God (cf. Gal. 2:19–20).

Those in authority must use their authority to serve. They must be slaves of justice and stewards of the divine law. Most importantly, their actions and words must attest to the justice and truth that God requires of all men. The consequence of their disobedience to these obligations is sin and chaos. If they do not act justly, serve those entrusted to them, and live as examples of truth, they will lead others astray and encourage sin. Their judgment will be severe (cf. Mt. 7:15; 18:6; Lk. 17:1; 1 Cor. 8:10–13).

The tremendous gift of freedom God gave us demands responsibility. The responsible use of human freedom has always required right order and conduct. Sin entered the world because of disobedience to a command of God. Death entered the world because of lawlessness. When the only law God gave Adam was struck down, death became the consequence for us all. Sacred Scripture teaches that we must choose to follow the Lord and all His commands and so live, or forsake Him in disobedience to His commands and die in sin. In short, we are known by the acts we perform. If we live in chaos and darkness, our father is Satan; if we live in right order and obedience to God's laws, we will share heaven's glory as children of God (cf. Lk. 6:45; Jn. 8:34–51).

Competent Authority

Because the right use of laws, and right order in society protect us from sin and encourage the grace of salvation, those in authority must use their authority wisely. Particularly in the Church, ecclesiastical laws can be a great blessing to the faithful if promulgated and enforced in a spirit of love and service.

It is not enough to have proper and good authority and laws; we also must follow them. Without laws to guide us, we are susceptible to our own imaginations and passions. As is evident in our world, one person's imagination and desires differ greatly from another's, thus causing chaos and conflict. Laws that govern proper living and regulate human affairs protect against chaos and conflict, thus protecting us from sin and death. If we are disobedient to the laws of justice, we could tempt our superiors to sin and fall prey to the curse of Adam. If we remain obedient for love of God and love of neighbor, we receive the fruits of the tree of life, Who is Christ Himself.

It would do us well to pray for those in authority (cf. 1 Tim. 2:1–4), for it is a well known fact that those in authority are not free from sin. Without love and a sincere desire to serve others, those in lawful authority can lose credibility. Likewise, we lose credibility when we wrongfully disobey lawful authority. If we follow the laws of the Church, we remain obedient to lawful authority and protect our consciences. Let us pray for each other, that we might remain obedient servants of God.

This chapter is based upon an article that first appeared in the July 9, 1997 issue of *Christifideles*, the newsletter of the St. Joseph Foundation. For more information about the St. Joseph Foundation, call 210–697–0717 or visit their Web site: www.st-joseph-foundation.org.

Questions for Reflection
or Group Discussion

1. What are the different types of laws? What images come to mind when I think of law? Do I think of laws as reflections of God's order, or as mere burdens and obligations?

2. Read Catechism, no. 1959. Why should human laws reflect the natural law? What happens when they don't?

3. What are the responsibilities of those in authority in the Church or society? What should my approach be to those in authority?

GETTING AWAY WITH MURDER?
THE CHURCH'S TEACHING ON CAPITAL PUNISHMENT

What is the Church's teaching on capital punishment?

"[T]he traditional teaching of the Church does not exclude recourse to the death penalty, if this is the only possible way of effectively defending human lives against the unjust aggressor.

"If, however, non-lethal means are sufficient to defend and protect people's safety from the aggressor, authority will limit itself to such means, as these are more in keeping with the concrete conditions of the common good and more in conformity with the dignity of the human person.

"Today, in fact . . . the cases in which the execution of the offender is an absolute necessity 'are very rare, if not practically non-existent' [John Paul II, *Evangelium vitae* 56]" (Catechism, no. 2267).

Framing the Discussion
Capital punishment has emerged as a significant social and political issue in recent decades. This development is largely the result of the serious problem of violent crime in the United States.

On this issue, Catholics are often divided along political lines: Political conservatives tend to favor capital punishment, while political liberals tend to oppose it. The Church teaches that the death penalty is not always and everywhere wrong. Whether our society can justly impose the death penalty is to a certain extent a prudential judgment on which there is room for some legitimate disagreement.

Should our political affiliation form our perspectives on the issue by default? No. Much of the disagreement on this subject arises because Catholics have not allowed themselves to be formed by the Church's teachings in their fullness.

Traditional Teaching

To understand the mind of the Church on this matter, we must begin with the principle that the Church's Magisterium, as the authentic interpreter of Scripture and Tradition, has never taught that capital punishment is intrinsically evil. Moreover, the Church has always recognized that the state has the authority, in certain circumstances, to impose the death penalty on one who has committed a capital offense. Thus, the Church distinguishes capital punishment from intrinsically evil acts like abortion and euthanasia, which ought never to be chosen and can never be legitimized by the state.[1]

Note, however, that we are merely saying that there is not a moral equivalence between abortion and the death penalty. It should be self-evident, however, that fundamental truths concerning the dignity and inviolability of human life should inform our thought on both topics. The Catechism, despite its well-publicized opposition to regular recourse to capital punishment, does not categorically condemn the practice. Rather, it affirms that in appropriate cases "the traditional teaching of the Church does not exclude recourse to the death penalty" (Catechism, no. 2267). This "traditional teaching" is found in the *Roman Catechism*, which was promulgated following the Council of Trent (1545–63):

> Another kind of lawful slaying belongs to the civil authorities, to whom is entrusted power of life and death, by the legal and judicious exercise of which they punish the guilty and protect the innocent. The just use of this power, far from involving the crime of murder, is an act of paramount obedience to [the Fifth] Commandment which prohibits murder. The end of the Commandment is the preservation and security of human life. Now the punishments inflicted by the civil authority, which is the legitimate avenger of crime, naturally tend to this end, since they give security to life by repressing outrage and violence.[2]

---

[1] Cf. Pope John Paul II, Encyclical Letter on the Value and Inviolability of Human Life *Evangelium Vitae* (March 25, 1995), nos. 62, 65, 73.
[2] John A. McHugh and Charles J. Callan, trans., "The Fifth Commandment," in *Catechism of the Council of Trent* (South Bend, Ind.: Marian Publications, 1972), 421.

This teaching also draws support from doctors of the Church. Saint Thomas Aquinas wrote that "if a man be dangerous and infectious to the community, on account of some sin, it is praiseworthy and advantageous that he be killed in order to safeguard the common good."[3] This teaching in turn can be traced back to the Sacred Scriptures. For Saint Paul teaches that civil government bears the sword as the agent of God's vengeance and therefore "is God's servant for your good" (Rom. 13:4).

Murder or Self-Defense?

Recognizing that the Church has always admitted that the death penalty can be a justifiable exercise of the state's authority, we now examine how this teaching fits in with the entire body of Church teaching. Ironically, capital punishment is always discussed under the general heading of the Fifth Commandment. ("Thou shalt not kill.") Killing another human being as an act of free will—as opposed to unintentional or accidental killing—is murder, and is always wrong (cf. Catechism, no. 2268). Since the criminal is indeed a human being, and his or her execution is an intentional act, it is fair to ask whether the execution is murder.

In recognizing the permissibility of capital punishment, the Church has always treated it as a kind of self-defense. If, for example, the only way I can immediately prevent someone from killing me or another person is by killing the aggressor, then I am morally permitted to do so. Such an act is not murder. How can this be? When a person kills another in self-defense, the immediate and proportionate good effect of saving one's own life justifies the action, even though there is also the evil effect of taking another's life (cf. Catechism, nos. 2263–64).

The Catechism teaches that "[l]egitimate defense can be not only a right but a grave duty for one who is responsible for the lives of others" (no. 2265). Pope John Paul II teaches that "[t]his is the context in which to place the problem of the *death penalty*."[4]

---

[3] Saint Thomas Aquinas, *Summa Theologiae*, IIa IIae, q. 64, art. 2; available from http://www.newadvent.org/summa/306402.htm.

[4] *Evangelium Vitae*, no. 56, emphasis in original.

The Catechism further recognizes that "[t]he defense of the common good requires that an unjust aggressor be rendered unable to cause harm" (no. 2265). This means that, at least in principle, capital punishment can be justified when used to protect society from an unjust aggressor.

As Pope John Paul II teaches in comparing capital punishment to abortion, "If such great care must be taken to respect every life, even that of criminals and unjust aggressors, the commandment 'You shall not kill' has absolute value when it refers to the innocent person."[5] For capital punishment to be licit, the intended good effect must be the protection of the common good, while the unintended—or tolerated—evil effect is the death of the criminal.

Changing Hearts

This understanding of the Church's rationale for historically teaching that the death penalty is permissible may come as a revelation to many. For example, some people hold that a person who commits a capital crime has forfeited his right to life, so the best he could hope for is the clemency of the state to stay the execution. In a sense this is true, just as an intruder has forfeited his right to life if I should be forced to kill him to protect my family from being harmed. But this forfeiture is not absolute. If I am able to protect my family by less drastic means, I should do so, and once the threat is over (when the intruder is apprehended and in jail), I no longer have the right to use deadly force.

Likewise, for capital punishment to be licit, it simply is not enough for someone to have committed a serious crime. If the preservation of the common good of society does not require it, then it cannot be justified because of the ever-present command, "Thou shalt not kill."

Further, we need to look at the primary reasons why we punish criminals. Our "culture of death" has largely given up on the possibility of reforming or rehabilitating (that is, converting) the criminal, despite the fact that "as far as possible,

---

[5] *Evangelium Vitae*, no. 57, emphasis in original.

[punishment] must contribute to the correction of the guilty party [cf. Lk. 23: 4–43]" (Catechism, no. 2266).

Some hold that the imposition of the death penalty helps lead to the repentance of criminals. An American bishops' document, in contrast, states, "It may be granted that the imminence of capital punishment may induce repentance in the criminal, but we should certainly not think that this threat is somehow necessary for God's grace to touch and to transform human hearts."[6] Likewise, Archbishops Charles Chaput of Denver, Eusebius Beltran of Oklahoma City, and Justin Rigali of St. Louis[7] stated in the aftermath of the Timothy McVeigh trial that the death penalty today serves to perpetuate the cycle of violence and diminish respect for human life, without providing authentic healing for the victims of crime.[8]

Deterrence and retribution are legitimate reasons for punishment in general, but they do not necessarily provide compelling reasons for capital punishment. It is indeed absolutely essential to redress the disorder caused by the offense and to ensure the safety of innocent citizens (cf. Catechism, no. 2266). But does capital punishment really do this?

The American bishops, while recognizing the historical validity of capital punishment, have consistently opposed capital punishment in the United States over the past twenty years, both individually and in conference documents: *Statement on Capital Punishment* (1980), *Confronting a Culture of Violence* (1994), and their 1996 statement on political responsibility, *Social Development and World Peace*. However, since this opposition is largely a prudential judgment on the part of the bishops, many American Catholics have ignored or rejected their teaching. Some have questioned whether the bishops' stance has been a fair reading of "the signs of the times . . . in the light of the Gospel."[9]

---

[6] U.S. Catholic Bishops, "USCCB Statement" (November 1980); available from www.usccb.org/sdwp/national/criminal/death/uscc80.htm.

[7] Now Cardinal Archbishop of Philadelphia.

[8] See http://www.archden.org/archbishop/docs/mcveigh_execution.htm; http://www.archden.org/archbishop/docs/violence.htm;andwww.mocatholic.org/view_article.asp?article_id=541.

[9] Second Vatican Council, Pastoral Constitution on the Church in the Modern World *Gaudium et Spes* (December 7, 1965), no. 4.

A Catholic Issue

Herein lies the importance of Pope John Paul II's encyclical *Evangelium Vitae*. Respecting the value and inviolability of all human life is not a conservative or liberal issue, but a Catholic issue. Of course, the Holy Father's treatment of capital punishment in this encyclical is subordinate to the treatment of abortion and euthanasia. Yet all these subjects trace back to what the Holy Father calls the Gospel of Life, which involves the proclamation of "the *incomparable value of every human person*."[10]

In *Evangelium Vitae*, the Holy Father observes that

> there is a growing tendency, both in the Church and in civil society, to demand that [the death penalty] be applied in a very limited way or even that it be abolished completely. The problem must be viewed in the context of a system of penal justice ever more in line with human dignity and thus, in the end, with God's plan for man and society. . . . Public authority must redress the violation of personal and social rights by imposing on the offender an adequate punishment for the crime, as a condition for the offender to regain the exercise of his or her freedom. In this way authority also fulfills the purpose of defending public order and ensuring people's safety, while at the same time offering the offender an incentive and help to change his or her behavior and be rehabilitated.[11]

It is clear that, for these purposes to be achieved, the nature and extent of the punishment must be carefully evaluated and decided upon, and ought not go to the extreme of executing the offender except in cases of absolute necessity: in other words, when it would not be possible otherwise to defend society. Today, however, as a result of steady improvements in the organization of the penal system over the centuries, such cases are very rare, if not practically non-existent.

The issue, then, is not merely the gravity of the crime; the Holy Father does not say "only in the case of especially heinous crimes," or "three strikes and you're out," or "use a gun, get the

---

[10] *Evangelium Vitae*, no. 2, emphasis in original.
[11] *Evangelium Vitae*, no. 56.

chair." Serious crimes obviously demand serious redress, but the death penalty, as the most extreme form of punishment, is reserved for those instances where society is unable otherwise to protect itself against the criminal. An example might be a serial murderer who regularly escapes from prison. But if society is able to protect itself without recourse to killing, is that not more in keeping with the civilization of life and love that Pope John Paul II is trying to promote?

After the release of *Evangelium Vitae*, Joseph Cardinal Ratzinger commented that

> "[t]he encyclical is concerned with the sacredness of man, and that is why the Pope insists that [the death penalty] be applied only to the most critical cases, and fervently hopes that it will be eventually abolished. . . . You ask about the correct interpretation of the teaching of the encyclical on the death penalty. *Clearly, the Holy Father has not altered the doctrinal principles which pertain to this issue as represented in the Catechism, but has simply deepened the application of such principles in the context of present-day historical circumstances.* Thus, where other means for the self-defense of society are possible and adequate, the death penalty may be permitted to disappear. Such a development, occurring within society and leading to the foregoing of this type of punishment, is something good and ought to be hoped for.[12]

Two years later, while visiting the United States, Pope John Paul II reiterated his plea that capital punishment be abolished: "I renew the appeal I made most recently at Christmas for a consensus to end the death penalty, which is both cruel and unnecessary."[13]

The *Catechism of the Catholic Church*, which incorporates the papal teaching on the death penalty found in *Evangelium Vitae*, Pope John Paul II, and the American Bishops have provided us with consistent teaching that is true to the deposit of the faith and also responsive to contemporary circumstances.

---

[12] As quoted in Richard John Neuhaus, "A Clarification on Capital Punishment," *First Things*, no. 56 (October 1995): 74–91, emphasis added.

[13] Pope John Paul II, Homily at Trans World Dome, St. Louis, Mo., (January 27, 1999).

Practical Applications of the Church's Teaching

Our proclamation of the Gospel of Life must be inclusive, consistent, and ultimately magnanimous. What does this mean? We must proclaim in season and out of season the right to life of the unborn. But our advocacy should not stop there. We also need to support mothers who, often through ignorance or seemingly unbearable circumstances, are tempted to consent to the killing of their own children.

We must defend the "right to life" of those in the abortion industry, converting hearts and never taking our lead from the misguided few who have resorted to violence. If a woman is pregnant as a result of rape, we should both affirm the human dignity and right to life of the child and offer support to the woman who has been victimized by this act of unspeakable violence. Part of being "pro-woman" in this instance means ensuring that the perpetrator of the crime is apprehended and punished.

And yet, we must go further and also recognize the human dignity—and capacity to be saved (cf. 1 Tim. 2:5)—of the rapist, who may well be very difficult to love, and very easy for society to discard. Following the lead of the late Mother Teresa of Calcutta, we must look for the hidden Jesus in the womb, in the hearth, in the convalescent hospital, in prison, and even on death row (cf. Mt. 25:31–46).

Perhaps this teaching on the death penalty can assist our efforts in other parts of the pro-life movement. Abortion is often distinguished from capital punishment because the unborn child is an "innocent" person.[14] Yet when we emphasize the word "innocent," we run a few risks. First, some might argue for a definition of "innocent" that would posit that the hardship or even inconvenience caused by an unwanted pregnancy disqualifies the baby from claiming "innocence." Second, we might come to see anyone who is not "innocent" as having lost his human dignity. Yet, as the Holy Father explains in *Evangelium Vitae*, "*Not even a murderer loses his personal dignity,*"

---

[14] Cf. Pope John Paul II, *Evangelium Vitae*, no. 57.

and God Himself pledges to guarantee this. And it is precisely here that the *paradoxical mystery of the merciful justice of God* is shown forth."[15]

The underlying basis for defending the right to life of the unborn baby is that he is a person created in the image and likeness of God and destined for eternal life. In a singular way, by becoming man, God has united Himself with every person and thus manifests the unique dignity and inviolability of all human life.[16] The "innocence" of the unborn child, in that he is neither an aggressor nor one who has ever committed actual sin, certainly strengthens his claim to life, but ultimately the weight of his claim resides in his humanity, not in his "innocence."

Applying the Church's teaching on capital punishment also enables us to resist negative labels. We are "pro-life," which is much more profound (and accurate) than simply being "anti-abortion." Similarly, it is not enough to be "anti-capital punishment." The goal should be to convert the criminal to Christ, and not simply to obtain a reprieve from the governor. And certainly we are not anti-capital punishment at the expense of not punishing crimes or safeguarding our society.

Some Catholics may be called to proclaim the Gospel of Life by engaging in prison ministry; we all could remember in our prayers those who are engaged in such ministry. All of us, too, can work to create a legal justice system—from the way our legislation is written, to the way trials are conducted, to the way prisons are operated—that respects the human dignity of the criminal, even when the criminal himself does not respect it. But even more fundamentally, all of us need to take a stand against the violence that so characterizes the culture of death, the violence that is largely the harvest of a society that has lost its sense of God.

---

[15] Pope John Paul II, *Evangelium Vitae*, no. 9, emphasis in original.
[16] Cf. Second Vatican Council, *Gaudium et Spes*, no. 22.

Unmasking the Culture of Death

I believe that capital punishment, as the Holy Father said in St. Louis, is both 'cruel and unnecessary.' In essence, it is really a mask that covers the deeper issue we as a society are afraid to face: the lack of respect for human life—particularly of the preborn, the disabled and the elderly. Only when we have the courage to remove that mask, will the sores hidden beneath it cease to fester. Only then will we—as individuals and as a society—begin the process of healing, moving away from a culture of death into a culture of life.[17]

—Archbishop Renato R. Martino

Questions for Reflection or Group Discussion

1. Where do I stand on the issue of capital punishment? How does the Church's teaching help to form my conscience on the subject?

2. How is capital punishment related to abortion? How do these two life issues differ?

3. Visiting those who are imprisoned is a corporal work of mercy and helping them turn their hearts to Christ is a spiritual work of mercy (cf. Mt. 25:31–46; Catechism, no. 2447). What can I do to advance the "Gospel of Life" among the imprisoned?

_____

[17] "Death Penalty Is Cruel and Unnecessary: Address at a Preparatory Meeting on the U.N. Resolution for a Moratorium on Capital Punishment," as quoted in *L'Osservatore Romano* (English ed., February 24, 1999), 2–3.

Chapter 11

COMING TO OUR CENSUS
DEBUNKING THE OVERPOPULATION MYTH

Is the world overpopulated? Could we not cure countless social problems if we stabilized or curbed the rate of population growth?

The claims of individuals and organizations like Zero Population Growth (ZPG) crumble in any encounter with the facts. Proponents of population control argue that the earth has too fragile an environment, too little space, and too few resources to sustain population growth. Historic and scientific facts prove these arguments false. More importantly, Sacred Scripture and the teachings of the Catholic Church on man's nature and the purpose of the earth provide a proper understanding of the issues and offer just solutions to the social problems of our day.

Overpopulation is frequently alleged to justify the promotion of contraception, abortion, and sterilization. It is said that poverty, crime, hunger, pollution, and a host of other evils stem from having too many people in the world. This worldview is treated as fact by many educational programs in public and private schools. American foreign policy often makes aid to developing nations dependent on their acceptance of population control measures.

Antinatalists—those who oppose population growth—promote abortion, contraception, sterilization, and sometimes even euthanasia and homosexual activity as means of regulating and curbing population growth. Because of the gravity of these issues, they deserve separate consideration.[1] It is not our purpose here to evaluate these means of population control, but rather to examine the assertions used to promote them—namely, that the world contains, or will soon contain, too many people—and refute these assertions with the truth.

---

[1] See CUF's FAITH FACTS on these issues, which may be obtained by calling CUF toll free at (800) MY-FAITH or by visiting www.cuf.org.

Concerns about the number of people on our planet date back to ancient times. Plato, Aristotle, and Saint Jerome are among those who voiced opinions on the subject. Modern discussion of the issue is generally traced to Thomas Malthus, who wrote a seminal essay on the problem of overpopulation in 1798.[2] However, it would be a great disservice to him to call contemporary antinatalists "neo-Malthusians." For all his concern about the relationship between available resources and the number of consumers, Malthus himself never advocated the coercive, contraceptive approach we associate with population planning today.

It took Margaret Sanger, founder of the American Eugenics League, to put the "control" in "birth control." Desiring to "escape the burden of unwanted children,"[3] she helped popularize abortion, contraception, and sterilization in our nation during the early part of the twentieth century.[4] Her ideology was known as eugenics, because its goal was the encouragement of a good gene pool (eugenics comes from Greek words that mean "good" and "gene"). Her ideas were similar to those of the Nazis; her own publication, *The Birth Control Review*, published articles written by members of the Nazi Party and other racist groups.[5] After Adolf Hitler showed the world what eugenics was really all about, Sanger's "birth control movement had to take a quick step away from its overt eugenical language," and it became Planned Parenthood.[6]

---

[2] Thomas Malthus, *An Essay on the Principle of Population* (New York: Dutton, 1967).

[3] Margaret Sanger, *Woman and the New Race* (New York: Truth Publishing, 1920); available from http://www.pro-life.net.

[4] Interestingly, these means of birth control were also promoted by Annie Wood Besant. In 1891, Besant succeeded Helena Petrovna as head of the Theosophic Society. Theosophic philosophies and practices are rooted in the occult and provide the substance of New Age belief. The Holy See condemned this philosophy in 1919. For more information, see chapter 21.

[5] Sanger published the first copy of *The Birth Control Review* in February of 1917 and continued its publication until May of 1923, when it was taken over by the American Birth Control League, which Sanger founded in 1921.

Cf. Ernst Rudin, "Eugenic Sterilization: An Urgent Need," *Birth Control Review* 17, no. 4 (April 1933), 102–104. Ernst Rudin was Hitler's director of genetic sterilization and a founder of the Nazi Society for Racial Hygiene.

[6] Elasah Drogin, *Margaret Sanger: Father of Modern Society* (New Hope, Ky.: CUL Publications, 1979), 29.

Conserving Room and Resources?

Believing that Jews and others were crowding them out, the National Socialists waged a world war to gain the *lebensraum* (living space) that Germans allegedly needed and deserved. Antinatalists today are declaring "World War III" on the growth rate of those groups they believe are less worthy of consuming the world's limited room and resources. As Jacqueline Kasun demonstrates in *The War against Population*, their contentions lack merit. We are not close to running out of anything.[7]

In fact, the vast majority of the planet's inhabitable surface is uninhabited. There are approximately 52.5 million square miles of land in the world, excluding Antarctica.[8] In 1998, the world's population was 5.9 billion.[9] By allowing 3.5 square feet per person, all the people in the world could be brought together in an area the size of the city of Jacksonville, Florida. While everyone would admittedly be cramped in Jacksonville, it would be possible to allot each individual person 1,000 square feet (4,000 square feet of living space for a family of four) and still fit the entire world's population in the states of Nebraska, Kansas, and South Dakota, leaving the rest of the United States, plus Canada, Mexico, Central and South America, Europe, Africa, Asia, and the Australian South Pacific areas completely uninhabited by man.[10] Thus, "[t]he feeling of the typical air passenger that he is looking down on a mostly empty earth is correct."[11]

Furthermore, there is little evidence that our resources are running out. Marshalling the available data, Kasun concludes that "there is very little probability of running out of anything essential to the industrial process at any time in the foreseeable

---

[7] Cf. Jacqueline Kasun, *The War against Population* (San Francisco: Ignatius Press, 1988), 37–42.

[8] *Atlas of the World* (New York: Oxford University Press, 1998), XIV.

[9] U.S. Census Bureau, World Population Profile: 1998-Highlights, available from http://www.census.gov/ipc/www/wp98001.html.

[10] Rick and Jan Hess, *A Full Quiver* (Brentwood, Tenn.: Wolgemuth & Hyatt Publishers, 1989), 72–77.

[11] Kasun, *The War Against Population*, 38.

future."[12] In fact, most of the depletion deadlines predicted by ZPG alarmists of the 60s and 70s already have passed. Where is the threatened global collapse? Evidently, the "population bomb"[13] was a dud.

Ruining the Environment?

Another favorite tactic of the antinatalism lobby is to pit population against the environment. Billions of people being born, they think, will be the undoing of the matrix of biological life.

Anyone who has ever been to the Fresh Kills Landfill (on Staten Island, New York), where piles of refuse stretch from horizon to horizon, will readily concede that pollution is a serious problem.[14] However, industrialization itself, and not the number of people per se, is responsible for environmental degradation. It is up to the beneficiaries of the Industrial Revolution—namely, all of us—to see to it that advances are preserved, and harmful effects controlled and even eliminated. Perhaps it would be more to the point, in other words, to use fewer Styrofoam cups rather than trying to control population by using more condoms.

Concurring with the antinatalists, many animal rights lobbyists argue that human beings are the dangerous foreign element to be purged from (or at least contained upon) an otherwise pristine planet. This idea is aptly demonstrated in an ACTION ALERT letter from the National Wildlife Federation (NWF): "Please write to your Representative and Senators, and tell them to support more money for family planning programs in the Foreign Operations Bill. Tell them to OPPOSE amendments that will restrict the delivery of safe, effective, voluntary family planning services. Someday humans and wildlife may be able to coexist in a peaceful balance, but

---

[12] Kasun, *The War Against Population*, 39.

[13] Paul R. Ehrlich, *Population Bomb* (New York: Ballantine Books, 1968).

[14] For more information on Catholic teaching on the stewardship of the environment, see Pope John Paul II, On Social Concern *Sollicitudo Rei Socialis* (December 30, 1987); available from http://www.osjspm.org/cst/srs_el.htm.

that day has not yet arrived. Stabilizing the human population is essential if we are to achieve that balance."[15]

This argument not only denies the privileged position man has over the lower creatures, it places him at a lower level of importance. While defining the human being as "the only animal that practices birth control,"[16] many groups like NWF contend that this one "animal" has no business surviving and thriving in this world. This view, however, requires that we ask this question: Do human beings belong exclusively to the natural world, or do they also belong to the supernatural? If we belong exclusively to the natural world, we have just as much right to exist as do snail darters and seals. The case is even more compelling when we consider man's supernatural calling, but most animal rights activists do not accept this premise. The possibility of a supernatural realm would require acceptance of man's primacy and demolish their worldview more surely than any environmental damage could demolish their world.

Consummate Consumer

For the overpopulation alarmist, the child is the consummate consumer. As one antinatalist ad of the 1970s put it: "Every 8 seconds a new American is born. He is a disarming little thing, but he will consume 26,000,000 gallons of water, 21,000 gallons of gasoline, 10,150 pounds of meat, 28,000 pounds of milk and cream, 9,000 pounds of wheat, and great storehouses of all other foods, drinks, and tobaccos."[17] No mention is made of the fact that this same child will also grow up to be a producer and contribute to society in tangible and intangible ways.

And what of the child who, because of handicap, injury, or inability, will simply not prove to be a major producer? In the wake of the Nazi experience, and now facing the modern reality

---

[15] National Wildlife Federation, "Action Alert" on Population (June 10, 1997), emphasis in original; available from http://www.nwf.org/action/.
[16] Paul R. Ehrlich, Anne H. Ehrlich, and Gretchen C. Daily, *The Stork and the Plow: The Equity Answer to the Human Dilemma* (New York: Putnam, 1995), 33.
[17] Lawrence Lader, *Breeding Ourselves to Death* (New York: Ballantine, 1971), 82.

of abortion and euthanasia, need we wonder any longer where the suppression of those whom the Nazis called the "useless eaters" finally leads?

Reducing World Hunger?

Although the "eliminating useless eaters" strategy was tried in this century and judged a crime against humanity, the antinatalists continue to advocate it when they address the problem of world hunger. They argue that to reduce world hunger, we must reduce the numbers of the hungry. "Pope denounces birth control as millions starve," trumpets an ad placed in *The New York Times* by the Campaign to Check the Population Explosion.[18] The ad was placed in response to the promulgation of Pope Paul VI's courageous encyclical, *Humanae Vitae*.

In our world, there is plenty of food, but it is poorly distributed. In a world where we have the potential to produce many times more food than we have already, should not we feed people rather than eliminate them? Pope Paul VI called for increasing economic development while rejecting contraception; Margaret Sanger thought the opposite. In her book *The Pivot of Civilization*, she argues that efforts to provide sustenance for the malnourished are wrongheaded, and that preventing people from starving to death will allow them to survive and procreate, thus producing more potential starvation victims, whom she also opposes feeding.[19] In retrospect, should not the ad's headline have read instead, "Margaret Sanger Denounces Feeding the Hungry as Millions Starve?"

Fundamentally Elitist Mentality

There is an old story about an antinatalist zealot attending a penthouse cocktail party. Holding forth at eloquent length on the need to reduce the number of people in the world, he was interrupted in his monologue by the hostess, who graciously

---

[18] Lader, *Breeding Ourselves to Death*, 66.
[19] Cf. Sanger, "The Cruelty of Charity," in *The Pivot of Civilization* (London: Butler and Tanner, 1923), 106–121.

ushered him to a nearby window. "If there are too many people in the world," she smiled, "why don't you go first?"

Proponents of population control are not arguing that there are too many people in the world. They are arguing that there are too many *other* people in the world. True to their eugenic roots, population alarmists divide the human race into the valuable part, which deserves to live, and the worthless part, which does not. The first tenet of their creed is that they themselves belong to the valuable, "good genes" group. In pitting population against natural resources, the environment, room on the planet, and available food, they simultaneously pit humanity against itself.

Catholic Objections to the Overpopulation Myth

The *means* and *goals* of population control proponents contradict the Catholic faith. The overpopulation myth fails to recognize three fundamental truths: the priceless value of each person, who is an immortal being made in the image and likeness of God (cf. Gen. 1:26–28); the universal destination of goods; and the preferential option for the poor.

While the antinatalists see and analyze a "population," the Christian knows that a population is a group—however large—of individual human beings. Each of us is endowed by God with an immortal soul. We are made in His image and likeness. Therefore, each person is not only more valuable than any earthly thing, but is valued on an entirely different scale. This truth makes population suppression repugnant, even if the claims of earthly amelioration were proven to be true. It would not be a Pyrrhic victory but a hellish defeat to wipe out world hunger by wiping out the hungry, to eradicate poverty by eradicating the poor. The hungry and poor are worth more than both their afflictions and the resources necessary to sustain them. Indeed, their own inestimable worth makes their afflictions worth addressing in the first place. Individuals are all valuable in the sight of God. Eugenic thinking is racist and directly opposed to the teachings of Christ.

While the antinatalists regard a baby as someone who wastes good food and resources, the Christian knows that sustaining human life is what food and resources are for. The notion that sustenance and raw materials should be hoarded for the privileged few by denying existence to the underprivileged contradicts the universal destination of goods. God intends this world's resources to be used by all people, not just by some. As the Catechism explains, "The goods of creation are destined for the whole human race" (no. 2402). The Catechism further teaches: "Goods of production . . . oblige their possessors to employ them in ways that will benefit *the greatest number*" (no. 2405, emphasis added).

When the antinatalists urge us to curb the births of less privileged humanity, they preach against every admonition of the Old and New Testaments on the subject of the poor. Scripture tells us the poor are the apple of God's eye and the proper object of our charity. The "preferential option for the poor"[20] (cf. Catechism, no. 2448) is a perennial aspect of Christian teaching. The antinatalist, on the other hand, could be described as having a "preferential option for the rich."

Paganism generally views new life with a critical eye, while the Judeo-Christian ethic sees children as a blessing from the Lord: "Your wife will be like a fruitful vine within your house; your children will be like olive shoots around your table. Lo, thus shall the man be blessed who fears the Lord" (Ps. 128:3–4).

God Himself took on flesh as a poor baby—bound to consume tons and tons of food, but also bound to set us free. The answer to this problem, as well as to the other problems of the modern world, is the Gospel of Jesus Christ. Spreading this Gospel is a vigorous and necessary task of the new evangelization, a task which Pope John Paul II has so often urged us to undertake.

---

[20] First Latin American Episcopal Conference (Medellin, 1968).

_____*SideBar*___

Modern Day Pharaohs

The pharaoh of old, haunted by the presence and increase of the children of Israel, submitted them to every kind of oppression and ordered that every male child born of the Hebrew women was to be killed (cf. Ex. 1:7–22). Today not a few of the powerful of the earth act in the same way. They too are haunted by the current demographic growth, and fear that the most prolific and poorest peoples represent a threat for the well-being and peace of their own countries. Consequently, rather than wishing to face and solve these serious problems with respect for the dignity of individuals and families and for every person's inviolable right to life, they prefer to promote and impose by whatever means a massive programme of birth control. Even the economic help which they would be ready to give is unjustly made conditional on the acceptance of an anti-birth policy.[21]

—Pope John Paul II

Questions for Reflection
or Group Discussion

1. How would I respond to someone who justifies contraception, abortion, or sterilization on the grounds that the world is already too crowded?

2. Do population control measures actually benefit the poor and the hungry? What are the fundamental differences between the Catholic Church and Planned Parenthood when it comes to addressing the issue of poverty?

3. Read Catechism, nos. 356–58 and 2415. Is the Church concerned about the environment? What is man's role with regard to the created world?

_____

[21] On the Value and Inviolability of Human Life *Evangelium Vitae* (March 25, 1995), no. 16.

Chapter 12

PLAY IT AGAIN
ORGAN DONATION

What is the position of the Catholic Church on organ donation for the purpose of transplant? Which moral principles are involved? What would motivate one to be an organ donor?

The Church teaches that "[a] particularly praiseworthy example of [the Gospel of Life] is the donation of organs, performed in an ethically acceptable manner."[1] Pope John Paul II sums up the teaching of the Church on organ donation in these words: "[T]he _Gospel of life_ is to be celebrated above all in _daily living_, which should be filled with self-giving love for others. . . . Over and above such outstanding moments, there is an everyday heroism, made up of gestures of sharing, big or small, which build up an authentic culture of life. A particularly praiseworthy example of such gestures is the donation of organs, performed in an ethically acceptable manner, with a view to offering a chance of health and even of life itself to the sick who sometimes have no other hope."[2]

There are different kinds of organ transplants, including inter vivos and postmortem (cadaver) transplants.[3] Inter vivos transplants refer to those that take place among the living. They would include a donation such as bone marrow. Postmortem transplants refer to donations given after death. These donations typically involve an organ necessary for sustaining life, such as a heart, lung, liver, or kidney.

---

[1] Pope John Paul II, Encyclical Letter on the Value and Inviolability of Human Life _Evangelium Vitae_ (March 25, 1995), no. 86.
[2] Pope John Paul II, _Evangelium Vitae_, no. 86, emphasis in original.
[3] Other types of transplants include _autografts, heterografts, static heterografts, static homografts,_ and _vital heterografts._ Definitions of these types of transplants can be found in Thomas O'Donnell, _Medicine and Christian Morality: Second Revised and Updated Edition_ (New York: Alba House, 1991), 118–22.

Ethical Considerations

Since the time of Pope Pius XII, the Church has explicitly taught that both types of transplants are licit, based upon the principle of fraternal charity, but only when certain requirements are met.

As the Catechism explains:

> *Organ transplants* are in conformity with the moral law if the physical and psychological dangers and risks to the donor are proportionate to the good that is sought for the recipient. Organ donation after death is a noble and meritorious act and is to be encouraged as an expression of generous solidarity. It is not morally acceptable if the donor or his proxy has not given explicit consent. Moreover, it is not morally admissible directly to bring about the disabling mutilation or death of a human being, even in order to delay the death of other persons (no. 2296, emphasis in original).

Inter Vivos Donations

In every instance, inter vivos transplants (vital homografts) raise serious ethical and moral questions. Because these donations require a transplant from one living person to another, a moral dilemma involving the principle of totality arises. According to this principle, the parts of the body are ordered to the good of that specific body. The surgical mutilation of a donor for the good of the recipient, therefore, must not seriously impair or destroy the bodily functions or bodily integrity of the donor.[4] For example, both eyes are necessary for certain visual functions. A living person would seriously impair his ability to see if he donated one of his eyes to another. Such a sacrifice would detract from the wholeness or full functioning of the donor's body. It would be a bad means to a good end, and therefore morally wrong.

Some argue that every person has a right over his own body and so may sacrifice his organs. They cite the examples of those, like Saint Maximilian Kolbe, who gave their lives to save another. This analogy, however, fails. Kolbe and others

---

[4] O'Donnell, *Medicine and Christian Morality*, 122.

freely accepted death, but did not choose death. They did not end their own life. Rather, these martyrs accepted death so as to save another's life. In contrast, an organ donor does choose to impair or destroy bodily functions within himself by transferring these functions, by means of transplant, to another.[5]

Based upon the law of fraternal charity, one may intend to sacrifice an organ for the sake of another, but one also has the responsibility for the integrity of one's body. Therefore, the principle of totality sets limits on inter vivos organ donations. Otherwise, inter vivos transplants could lead to suicide, or even euthanasia.

Postmortem Donations

The moral issues surrounding postmortem donations center around the definition of death. For a postmortem donation to be morally acceptable, those involved must have certain proof that death has occurred. It is immoral to cause the death of a donor by means of organ transplant, even if death from natural causes is inevitable. Thus, organ donation, even with the informed consent of the donor or his next of kin, is immoral if it violates the prohibition of removing vital organs from living persons, or if there is a false diagnosis of death for a person in an unconscious, "persistent vegetative state," or in a brain-resting state. Organ transplants under these conditions open the door to organ removal from patients with severely disabling conditions.

To protect against these dangers, three conditions must be met to justify a postmortem donation:

1. The donor must be verifiably and legitimately dead;
2. Proper, informed consent must have been given by the deceased donor with verification from a trustworthy source (in the absence of previous consent by the donor, consent of next of kin is permissible, provided that the deceased would not have opposed it); And

---

[5] Germain Grisez, *Living a Christian Life* (Quincy, Ill.: Franciscan Press, 1993), vol. 2, 543–44.

3. The remains of the donor must be treated with the same respect consistent with what was until death, and will be again, a temple of the Holy Spirit.[6]

The United States Conference of Catholic Bishops offers further guidelines for enforcing these ethical conditions: "The determination of death should be made by the physician or competent medical authority in accordance with responsible and commonly accepted scientific criteria. . . . [O]rgans should not be removed until it has been medically determined that the patient has died. In order to prevent any conflict of inter-est, the physician who determines death should not be a mem-ber of the transplant team."[7]

A Culture of Death

Powerful medical organizations that advocate organ dona-tion do not always support the morally correct position. Take, for example, the flip-flop stance of the Council on Ethical and Judicial Affairs of the American Medical Association. In 1988, the council concluded that it is "ethically acceptable" to use organs from anencephalic[8] infants *only after they have died.*[9] In 1994, the same council reversed its position by stating that it is ethically acceptable to transplant the organs of anencephalic infants *even before they die.*[10]

The rationale for the reversal, which includes the caveat that its position is still illegal in most jurisdictions, was pub-lished in a council report entitled "The Use of Anencephalic

---

[6] O'Donnell, *Medicine and Christian Morality*, 69.

[7] United States Conference of Catholic Bishops, "Ethical and Religious Directives for Catholic Health Care Services, Fourth Edition" (June 15, 2001), nos. 62, 64; available from www.nccbuscc.org/bishops/directives.htm.

[8] An anencephalic infant has a congenital absence of the cranial vault with cerebral hemispheres missing or reduced to small masses, together with other deformities. After delivery at term, the infant usually survives only a few minutes, sometimes a few hours, and rarely a few days.

[9] Council on Ethical and Judicial Affairs (CEJA), "Anencephalic Neonates as Organ Donors" (December 1988); CEJA reports available from www.ama-assn.org/ama/pub/category/3886.html.

[10] CEJA, "The Use of Anencephalic Neonates as Organ Donors" (December 1994).

Neonates as Organ Donors." The council based its changed stance upon the following justifications:

—There is a shortage of organs available for transplant in infants and young children.
—Anencephalic neonates lack functioning cerebral hemispheres and never experience any degree of consciousness.
—The benefits of such transplants will include saving some infants from death and substantially improve the quality of life of many others.
—Grieving parents of an anencephalic child will find some meaning in their tragedy if another child is allowed to benefit from a transplant.[11]

The Council on Ethical and Judicial Affairs (CEJA) argued that if the infant is deformed and lacks almost all brain tissue, he is only doubtfully human. However, such speculation is irrelevant in the Catholic context. There is no doubt whatsoever that this neonate is fully a human person. Nonetheless, the CEJA's "doubts" as to whether such an infant is human included the willingness to destroy it even if it is human. Thankfully, in 1995, the Council returned again to the 1988 guideline. However, the 1994 position shows a willingness to accept a utilitarian definition of life.[12] "Is it even a question of medicine to ask, much less answer, which life (or lives) have no value in themselves but only for others?"[13] Both law and ethics require that a person be dead before his vital organs be taken.

Promoting the Gospel of Life
The argument about anencephalic infants is important because it serves to show the progress made by the anti-life movement not only within the medical profession, but also

---

[11] *Journal of American Medical Association* (JAMA) vol. 273, no. 20, 1614–18.
[12] Cf. CEJA, "Anencephalic Infants as Organ Donors-Reconsideration" (December 1995).
    For the current policy of the AMA, see "Code of Medical Ethics," E-2.162; available from http://www.ama-assn.org/ad-com/polfind/ethics.pdf.
[13] Msgr. Wm. B. Smith, "Questions Answered," *Homiletic & Pastoral Review* (November 1995), 69–71.

within our society as a whole. Our current culture, dubbed the "culture of death" by Pope John Paul II, is echoing ideas similar to those in Germany before the Nazi regime took power. A culture that makes the choice to select which of its members is, or is not, worthy of life is playing God. To make such a choice implies that individuals of a society have value only insofar as their life is useful to the whole society. When an individual's life no longer is considered useful, then only his body parts, and not the person as a whole, have value. If this thinking continues to spread, it is only a matter of time until the laws of our country in every jurisdiction embrace euthanasia and assisted suicide as permissible.

In order to protect their own lives and promote the Gospel of Life for all, organ donors and those who survive them have a grave responsibility to practice and promote the moral teachings of the Church. If you are a card-carrying organ donor or in charge of deciding whether someone's organs ought to be donated or removed, be sure to discuss the moral principles of organ donation with your family, and consider including them in written directives. Organ donation is justifiable because of the principle of fraternal charity, but within the limits of the principle of totality. Within these limits, organ donation can witness to the Gospel of Life.

Questions for Reflection or Group Discussion

1. What is the principle of totality? What does it have to do with the morality of organ transplants?

2. The Church heartily approves of organ transplants when they are performed in an ethically acceptable manner. Why?

3. What sorts of transplants would be morally acceptable? What would render the other transplants immoral?

Chapter 13

Drawing the Line
The Church's Teaching on
Embryonic Stem Cell Research

What are stem cells? What does the Church teach about embryonic stem cell research?

Stem cells are the building blocks of human tissues. The Church teaches that the intentional destruction of human embryos, which is necessary for embryonic stem cell research, is gravely immoral (cf. Catechism, no. 2274–75).

Stem cells have two characteristics that make them *stem* cells. First, they can reproduce without becoming differentiated or specialized. Examples of differentiated cells are nerve, muscle, and blood cells. Second, stem cells can produce other cells, called progenitor cells, which can eventually spawn highly differentiated cells. In other words, a stem cell can produce a cell that can become the "ancestor" of a lineage of cells that produce muscle or blood cells. The progenitor cells and the lineages of cells they produce are together called stem cell lines.

Stem cells can be extracted from living human embryos or from the tissues of those who have been born, including the tissues of a mother's placenta. The former type of extraction for the purposes of research is called embryonic stem cell research; the latter, adult stem cell research.

Embryonic stem cell research involves several stages. First, embryos are obtained for experimentation, either by being deliberately brought to life for this purpose, or by using already living embryos. In either case, these embryos have been brought to life through in vitro fertilization—the fertilization of an egg by a sperm cell outside the human body—and may have been frozen for some time.

Second, the fertilized eggs divide and develop from one cell to blastocysts of at least thirty-two cells. Ordinarily, the development of a human being from his first stage of life (as a fertilized egg) to the blastocyst stage occurs during the first four or five days of life.

Third, the embryoblast, or inner cell mass, of the blastocyst is removed by the researcher. This removal of the embryoblast kills the embryo.

Fourth, the embryoblast is placed on irradiated mouse cells; here the human cells are cultured and multiply.

Fifth, human cell lines are harvested; these cell lines eventually differentiate into nerve, blood, and other cell lines.

Stem cells can be classified as totipotent, pluripotent, or multipotent stem cells. *Totipotent* stem cells can differentiate into all of the various stem cell lines. *Pluripotent* stem cells have the capacity to differentiate into most human tissues. Embryonic stem cells obtained from embryoblasts are pluripotent. *Multipotent* stem cells can differentiate into more specialized stem cell lines. Adult blood stem cells, for example, can become red blood cells, white blood cells, or platelets. Recently, pluripotent adult stem cells have been discovered in the brain, bone marrow, umbilical cord blood, and in other organs. The distinction among the types of stem cells is important because multipotent cells are the least versatile of the three and can potentially treat the fewest number of diseases.

The Promise of Stem Cell Research

Stem cells, according to scientific consensus, hold promise for restoring the tissues of people who suffer from Alzheimer's or Parkinson's disease, diabetes, and other debilitating illnesses. For example, insulin-producing cells developed from stem cells potentially could cure some forms of diabetes. Nerve cells developed from stem cells potentially could mitigate the effects of paralysis from spinal injuries.

Currently, a majority (but not a consensus) of scientists believes that embryonic stem cells hold more promise than adult stem cells for the treatment of such conditions. Embryonic stem cells exist in greater quantities and multiply more rapidly than adult stem cells.

The much-touted promise of embryonic stem cell research, however, is not yet a reality—embryonic stem cells, as of the time of the writing of this FAITH FACT, have yet to help a single human patient. "There is no evidence of therapeutic benefit from embryonic stem cells," according to Marcus Grompe, M.D., Ph.D., of the department of molecular and medical genetics of Oregon Health Sciences University.[1] Dr. Bert Vogelstein, professor of oncology and pathology at Johns Hopkins University, states that the promise of embryonic stem cell research is merely "conjectural."[2]

Adult stem cells, in contrast, are *currently* being used to help patients who suffer from the following conditions: (1) cancer, including brain tumors, retinoblastoma, ovarian cancer, solid tumors, testicular cancer, multiple myeloma and leukemias, breast cancer, neuroblastoma, non-Hodgkin's lymphoma, and renal cell carcinoma; (2) autoimmune diseases, including multiple sclerosis, lupus, juvenile rheumatoid arthritis, and rheumatoid arthritis; (3) stroke; (4) immunodeficiencies; (5) anemia; (6) cartilage and bone damage; (7) corneal scarring; (8) blood and liver disease; and (9) heart damage.[3]

Advances in biology have proven that a new human being exists with his own well-defined genetic identity at the moment of fertilization. From that point forward, the individual will develop gradually and continuously into a mature human being.

At the moment the human being begins to exist, he has a right to life (cf. Catechism, no. 2270). Every medical intervention on a human embryo that does not seek to benefit that particular human being is morally illicit.[4] For these reasons, the

---

[1] "Stem Cells and the Future of Regenerative Medicine," Workshop sponsored by National Academy of Sciences' Institute of Medicine, (Washington, D.C.: June 22, 2001), quoted in United States Conference of Catholic Bishops, Secretariat for Pro-Life Activities, "Current Clinical Use of Adult Stem Cells to Help Human Patients"; available from http://www.usccb.org/prolife/issues/bioethic/adult701.htm.

[2] "Stem Cells and the Furture of Regenerative Medicine," quoted in United States Conference of Catholic Bishops, "Current Clinical Use of Adult Stem Cells to Help Human Patients."

[3] United States Conference of Catholic Bishops, "Current Clinical Use of Adult Stem Cells to Help Human Patients."

[4] Cf. Congregation for the Doctrine of the Faith, Instruction on Respect for Human Life in Its Origin and on the Dignity of Procreation *Donum Vitae* (February 22, 1987), sec. I, no. 3.

Church teaches that the removal of the inner cell mass of the blastocyst, which kills a human being in his embryonic stage, is a gravely immoral act, whether the embryo was brought to life for this specific purpose or whether the embryo already exists.[5]

No intention, however good, can justify the killing of an innocent human being. Even if human embryonic stem cell research could one day provide relief for those who suffer from debilitating illnesses, the killing of one human embryo for this purpose could never be justified.[6]

Suppose, however, a researcher were not *directly* involved in the killing of the embryos. Could his participation in embryonic stem cell research be justified?

If his cooperation were formal, the answer is clearly no. Formal cooperation is the willing or intentional cooperation in an act committed by the principal agent, or doer, of the act. Formal cooperation in an evil, like embryonic stem cell research, is always immoral, much as the accomplice in a bank robbery who does not rob the bank but drives the getaway car commits an immoral act.

Suppose, however, that researcher does not approve of the gravely immoral acts by which embryonic stem cells are produced, and intends to conduct research on already existing embryonic stem cell lines for the benefit of humanity. Would his cooperation be morally permissible?

The bishops of the United States, as well as the Pontifical Academy for Life, say no. The pontifical academy believes such acts constitute proximate material cooperation in the evils of in vitro fertilization and the killing of embryos: "Is it morally licit to use ES [embryonic stem] cells, and the differentiated cells obtained from them, which are supplied by other researchers or are commercially obtainable? The answer is negative, since: prescinding from the participation—formal or otherwise—in the morally illicit intention of the principal agent, the case in question entails a proximate material coop-

---

[5] Cf. Pontifical Academy for Life, "Instruction on the Production and the Scientific and Therapeutic Use of Human Embryonic Stem Cell Lines" (August 25, 2000).
[6] Cf. Pontifical Academy for Life, "Use of Human Embryonic Stem Cell Lines."

eration in the production and manipulation of human embryos on the part of those producing or supplying them."[7]

Embryonic stem cell research on existing stem cell lines is also immoral because the embryos never consented to the research. Even if the parents consented to the research, such consent would be gravely immoral because the research does not benefit the child but, on the contrary, kills the child. The Catechism teaches: "Experimentation on human beings is not morally legitimate if it exposes the subject's life or physical and psychological integrity to disproportionate or avoidable risks. Experimentation on human beings does not conform to the dignity of the person if it takes place without the informed consent of the subject or those who legitimately speak for him" (no. 2295). Parents who consent to embryonic stem cell research on their children do not legitimately speak for their children because such consent kills the child. While parents under ordinary circumstances legitimately speak for their children, they fail to do so when they consent to their children's homicide.

Moreover, embryonic stem cell research on existing stem cell lines is immoral because it is contrary to the dignity owed to the bodies of the deceased: "The bodies of the dead must be treated with respect and charity, in faith and hope of the Resurrection. The burial of the dead is a corporal work of mercy [cf. Tob. 1:16–18]; it honors the children of God, who are temples of the Holy Spirit" (Catechism, no. 2300). As the Congregation for the Doctrine of the Faith has taught, "The corpses of human embryos and fetuses, whether they have been deliberately aborted or not, must be respected just as the remains of other human beings. . . . Furthermore, the moral requirements must be safeguarded that there be no complicity in deliberate abortion and that the risk of scandal be avoided. Also, in the case of dead fetuses, as for the corpses of adult persons, all commercial trafficking must be considered illicit and should be prohibited."[8]

---

[7] Pontifical Academy for Life, "Use of Human Embryonic Stem Cell Lines."
[8] Congregation for the Doctrine of the Faith, *Donum Vitae*, sec. I, no. 4.

By Their Fruits You Will Know Them

Embryonic stem cell research is a poisonous fruit of in vitro fertilization. The Church teaches that in vitro fertilization, even when the donors of the sperm and the egg are married, "is in itself illicit and in opposition to the dignity of procreation and of the conjugal union, even when everything is done to avoid the death of the human embryo."[9]

In vitro fertilization is gravely immoral because it destroys "the inseparable connection, established by God, which man on his own initiative may not break, between the unitive significance and the procreative significance which are both inherent to the marriage act."[10] Contraception is always immoral because it excludes the conjugal act's procreative meaning. In vitro fertilization is always immoral because it excludes the conjugal act's unitive meaning.

In vitro fertilization, moreover, is ordinarily attended by the grave moral evil of masturbation (cf. Catechism, no. 2352).

Embryonic stem cell research, then, is gravely immoral because it necessarily involves the killing of an innocent human being. Adult stem cell research is already helping patients who suffer from nearly two dozen conditions. The former should be shunned and the latter pursued, to the glory of God.

Questions for Reflection or Group Discussion

1. What is a stem cell?

2. What are the different types of stem cells?

3. Why is embryonic stem cell research immoral?

---

[9] Congregation for the Doctrine of the Faith, *Donum Vitae*, sec. II, no. 5.

[10] Pope Paul VI, Encyclical on the Regulation of Birth *Humanae Vitae* (July 25, 1968), no. 12.

Chapter 14

WHAT MAKES A MARRIAGE?
CONSENT, CONSUMMATION, AND
THE SPECIAL CASE OF THE HOLY FAMILY

Must a marriage be consummated in order to be valid? Can a valid marriage be dissolved? If so, what about the marriage of Joseph and Mary, which was not consummated?

A marriage is valid when both parties have expressed their free consent to be married through the exchange of vows, even though they have not consummated their union. However, a marriage that has not been consummated may be dissolved by the Church.[1]

Joseph and Mary's complete commitment to doing the will of God made the dissolution of their marriage a nonissue once Joseph learned of the supernatural circumstances surrounding Mary's pregnancy (cf. Mt. 1:18–25). As Pope John Paul II has written, "In the course of that pilgrimage of faith which was his life, Joseph, like Mary, remained faithful to God's call until the end."[2]

Free Gift of Self

For a marriage to be valid, two persons must enter into the covenant with free and mutual consent: They must enter into the marriage covenant while "not being under constraint" and "not impeded by any natural or ecclesiastical law" (Catechism, no. 1625). The Church teaches that this free exchange of consent is the indispensable element necessary for a valid marriage.

---

[1] Cf. *Code of Canon Law* (Washington, D.C.: Canon Law Society of America, 1983), can. 1142.

[2] Pope John Paul II, Apostolic Exhortation on the Person and Mission of Saint Joseph in the Life of Christ and of the Church *Redemptoris Custos* (August 15, 1989), no. 17.

While it is not necessary for a marriage to be consummated in order to be valid, a marriage that has not been consummated by the spouses may be dissolved by the Church; either spouse of a non-consummated marriage may seek to have the marriage dissolved. However, a valid, consummated marriage "between baptized persons can never be dissolved" (Catechism, no. 1640).

Today, we rarely find married couples who do not plan to consummate their union. The Church usually recommends that those who desire to live in a state of consecrated virginity enter a religious order or live alone. Even so, there are examples of "Josephite" marriages throughout Church history—marriages in which the spouses, in imitation of Joseph and Mary, express their mutual love while offering their virginity or celibacy as a fruitful witness to the Kingdom of God and the future resurrection. The Church has always defended the rights of couples who receive this unique charism, without in any way denigrating the vast majority of couples who do in fact consummate their marriage (cf. 1 Cor. 7:36–38).[3]

Holy Family

What, then, of Mary and Joseph? First, contrary to the views of some, they were in fact married, not engaged, *before* the angel told Joseph to take Mary into his home. In Jewish law, to be "betrothed" meant they were already married, even though they were not yet living together (cf. Lk. 1:26–38). Betrothal involved free and mutual consent, and thus constituted a valid marriage, as Pope John Paul II notes:

> Addressing Joseph through the words of the angel, God speaks to him as the husband of the Virgin of Nazareth. What took place in her through the power of the Holy Spirit also confirmed in a special way the marriage bond which already existed between Joseph and Mary. God's messenger was clear in what he said to Joseph: "Do not fear to take Mary your wife

---

[3] Cf. Pope John Paul II, Apostolic Exhortation on the Role of the Christian Family in the Modern World *Familiaris Consortio* (November 22, 1981), no. 16.

into your home." Hence, what had taken place earlier, namely, Joseph's marriage to Mary, happened in accord with God's will and was meant to endure. In her divine motherhood Mary had to continue to live as "a virgin, the wife of her husband" (cf. Lk. 1:27).[4]

For Mary and Joseph, doing God's will necessarily implied a marriage in which Mary would remain a virgin, a marriage of complete and holy continence for the husband and the wife. Their marriage is an exception in God's divine plan, yet they are truly a model for all married couples. Mary is a model because she always perfectly did God's will, and Joseph is an exemplar of "complete self-sacrifice" by taking Mary into his home, "while respecting the fact that she belonged exclusively to God."[5]

Marriage as Mission

"Patterned after the marvelous example of Joseph and Mary, every married couple is called to create a 'holy family' with Jesus as its center. In calling the family the domestic Church, the Church recognizes the fact that every married couple has a significant role to play in the Church. Their 'partnership of life and love' forms a microcosm of the Church and bears much-needed witness to a society hungering for Good News."[6]

"Part of the mission of the domestic Church is to raise godly children,"[7] or, in more formal language, "the procreation and education of children."[8] In other words, the family is called to welcome new members into the Kingdom of God. This mission is often linked, but not necessarily, to the fruit of sexual intercourse. In a broader sense, it can include adoption, foster parenting, acts of hospitality, and myriad forms of active

---

[4] Pope John Paul II, *Redemptoris Custos*, no. 18.
[5] Pope John Paul II, *Redemptoris Custos*, no. 20.
[6] Leon J. Suprenant, Jr., "The 'Real Presence' of the Marriage Bond," in *Catholic for a Reason: Scripture and the Mystery of the Family of God* (Steubenville, Ohio: Emmaus Road, 1998), 257–258.
[7] Suprenant, *Catholic for a Reason*, 258.
[8] Second Vatican Council, Pastoral Constitution on the Church in the Modern World *Gaudium et Spes* (December 7, 1965), no. 48.

apostolate (cf. Catechism, no. 1654). It follows that periodic or total abstinence from marital relations for the good of the Church—if it is the will of both spouses—is a sacrifice pleasing to God. Surely this was the case with Joseph and Mary, who faithfully placed themselves and their marriage at the service of the Incarnation and uniquely bore witness to the mystery of the Church, which is both Virgin and Spouse.[9]

Questions for Reflection or Group Discussion

1. The Church affirms that Joseph and Mary were true husband and wife, even though they never had marital relations. In what ways did Saint Joseph manifest his spousal love for Mary?

2. Spouses confer on each other the Sacrament of Matrimony when they publicly exchange their vows. Too often today, spouses are not faithful to their solemn promises. What does the example of Joseph and Mary teach us about marital fidelity? What counsel does the Church offer to married couples to live out their marriage vows? (See Catechism, nos. 1641–42.)

3. In the face of widespread divorce in contemporary Western society, the Church continues to maintain the timeless truth that a valid, consummated, sacramental marriage cannot be dissolved for any reason. How would I explain this teaching to someone who advocates divorce and remarriage? (See Catechism, nos. 2382–86.)

---

[9] Cf. Pope John Paul II, *Redemptoris Custos*, nos. 20–21.

Chapter 15

WHAT GOD HASN'T JOINED
THE ANNULMENT PROCESS

What is a declaration of nullity?

A declaration of nullity is not a divorce. A divorce ends the common life of an existent marriage. A declaration of nullity is a decree by a Church court stating that a marriage never existed. In a case of marriage nullity, the judges must determine whether the minimum requirements of marriage were met—not whether the ideal marriage was achieved. If the minimum requirements were met, the validity of the marriage is upheld.

Many people explain marriage nullity (an "annulment") as being a statement by the Church that a particular union was not a sacramental marriage and was thus invalid. That explanation is misleading and has no basis in Church teaching. If a marriage occurs, it is either a sacramental marriage or a natural marriage, but both are marriages, and both are recognized as valid by the Church. If the minimum requirements of either kind of marriage are met, the Church can uphold its validity. The fact that a marriage lacks sacramental dignity does not constitute grounds for invalidity.[1]

To understand declarations of nullity, we must know the general reasons for a declaration, the roles of the people involved, and the basic procedures used.

---

[1] A marriage is a sacrament if the husband and wife are baptized. It does not matter to which Christian community they belong. If one or both parties are not baptized, the marriage is not a sacrament, but is called a natural marriage [cf. *Code of Canon Law* (Washington, D.C.: Canon Law Society of America, 1983), can 1055 § 2; *Code of Canons of the Eastern Churches* (Washington, D.C.: Canon Law Society of America, 1990), hereafter CCEO, can. 776 §2].

Grounds for Marriage Nullity

Consent makes a marriage. As stated in canon law, "[T]he consent of the parties, legitimately manifested between persons who are capable according to law of giving consent, makes marriage; no human power is able to supply this consent."[2]

Thus, if one proves that consent was never legitimately exchanged, then one proves that the marriage never existed. Once consent is validly exchanged, a marriage occurs. If one of the spouses breaks the marriage vows, this does not "nullify" the marriage. Such acts are gravely sinful, but do not invalidate an otherwise valid marriage.

Another way to explain marital consent is by analogy to the sacraments. Every sacrament must have proper form and matter to be valid. For the Sacrament of the Eucharist, the proper form is the words of consecration spoken by a priest. The proper matter is wheat bread and grape wine. When the words of consecration are prayed, the bread and wine become the Body and Blood of Jesus. If someone takes the Sacred Host and breaks It into pieces, It remains the Body of Christ. Furthermore, if the priest later decides he does not believe in the Real Presence, his lack of faith does not affect the Eucharistic Presence of our Lord in the consecrated Hosts in the tabernacle.

In the same way, marriage has proper form and matter. The form is the words and rituals used to exchange consent. The proper matter for marriage is the man and woman capable of giving consent. Once the marriage vows are legitimately exchanged, the marriage occurs and remains, even if the vows are broken, or the spouses believe the marriage is dead.

To prove consent was never legitimately exchanged, one of three things must be established: the proper form of marriage was not used, one or both of the parties were incapable of exchanging consent, or consent itself was not exchanged.

---

[2] *Code of Canon Law*, can. 1057 §1; see also CCEO, can. 817.

Form of Marriage

The form of marriage refers to the wedding ceremony, the ritual used to exchange consent. Catholics must follow the Catholic form of marriage. Even if only one of the parties is Catholic, the Catholic form must be followed.[3]

For Catholics belonging to one of the Latin Rites, the form requires that consent be exchanged in the presence of a cleric, in accordance with the approved liturgical rite, and witnessed by two other people.[4] The cleric assisting at the wedding must have the proper authority to witness the marriage in the name of the Church. Under certain circumstances, when a genuine shortage of priests and deacons exists, members of the lay faithful can receive delegation from the diocesan bishop to assist at marriages.[5]

In the Eastern Catholic Churches, the required form is different: "Only those marriages are valid which are celebrated with a sacred rite, in the presence of the local hierarch, local pastor, or a priest who has been given the faculty of blessing the marriage by either of them, and at least two witnesses."[6]

The "sacred rite" means the assistance and blessing of a priest.[7] Contrary to the discipline of the Church in the West, the nuptial blessing is required for validity in the Eastern Catholic Churches. A deacon cannot assist at a marriage because he cannot give the nuptial blessing. If an Eastern Catholic contracts marriage with a member of an Eastern Orthodox Church according to the laws of the Orthodox Church, but without the permission of the Catholic hierarch, the marriage is valid if the nuptial blessing was given by a priest.[8]

In certain situations, the local ordinary or hierarch may dispense from the required form of marriage. If a Catholic, however, attempts marriage and neglects the proper form of marriage, the marriage is invalid.

---

[3] Cf. *Code of Canon Law*, can. 1059.
[4] Cf. *Code of Canon Law*, cann. 1108, 1119.
[5] Cf. *Code of Canon Law*, can. 1112.
[6] CCEO, can. 828 §1.
[7] Cf. CCEO, can. 828 §2.
[8] Cf. CCEO, can. 834 §2.

Diriment Impediments

A diriment impediment is a situation or condition that makes a person incapable of entering marriage.[9] If a diriment impediment exists, no marriage is contracted, even if consent is exchanged.

Before a priest witnesses a marriage, he is obligated to investigate the couple's situation and make certain no impediments exist.[10] This investigation is usually completed through a prenuptial questionnaire and a review of legal documents such as birth and baptismal certificates.

Some impediments are established by ecclesiastical law. They refer only to Catholics and are disciplines imposed for the right order of the sacraments and married life. In certain circumstances, these impediments can be dispensed. Other impediments are established by divine law and cannot be dispensed. These impediments apply to Catholics and non-Catholics alike.

Examples of diriment impediments that can be dispensed include marriage with a non-baptized person, consanguinity in the collateral line (marriage with a cousin), and legal relationship arising from adoption. Examples of diriment impediments that cannot be dispensed include antecedent and perpetual impotence, the bond of a previous marriage, and affinity in the direct line (that is, marriage with a parent or grandparent).[11]

Marital Consent

If the form of marriage is properly observed and no impediments exist, each of the parties in a marriage must still give free consent. If one or both do not give consent, a marriage never occurs. In general, there are three categories of defective consent: defects of knowledge, conditioned consent, and defects of will.[12] Each category contains several specific grounds for finding a lack of consent.

[9] Cf. *Code of Canon Law*, can. 1073; CCEO, can. 790.
[10] Cf. *Code of Canon Law*, can. 1066; CCEO, can. 785.
[11] For reference to these and the other diriment impediments, see the *Code of Canon Law*, cann. 1073–94; CCEO, cann. 790–812.
[12] Specific grounds of nullity that affect consent can be found in the *Code of Canon Law*, cann. 1095–1107; CCEO, cann. 817–27.

Generally speaking, defects of knowledge refer to situations in which one or both people do not have the necessary knowledge to choose marriage in their specific situation. For example, canon 1097 §1 reads: "Error concerning the person renders a marriage invalid." This means that if Jacob intends to marry Rachel, but her sister, Leah, wears a bridal veil and he mistakenly marries her instead, the marriage is invalid.[13]

Conditioned consent refers to a person qualifying his or her consent or placing conditions that violate the minimum requirements of marriage. A person not intending to have children is an example of conditioned consent. Children are a gift from God and, by divine law, all marriages must remain open to children. Specifically excluding children at the time of consent invalidates the consent.[14]

A defect of will occurs when a person marries against his or her will. Force and grave fear are examples of grounds for this category of invalidity.[15]

The judges hearing the case determine what the ground of nullity will be. They assess the grounds after reviewing the information given them by the petitioner and the responses offered by the respondent. If the minimum requirements to enter marriage were met, the marriage occurred, and no declaration of nullity should be given.

People Involved

There are three principal parties involved in the process of investigating marriage nullity. A *petitioner* is the person who files for the declaration of nullity. A *respondent* is the other spouse in the marriage under review. The *defender of the bond* is a person appointed by the court to defend the marriage bond. He "is bound by office to propose and explain everything which reasonably can be brought forth against nullity or dissolution."[16]

---

[13] The grounds of nullity referring to defects of knowledge can be found in the *Code of Canon Law*, cann. 1095–1100; CCEO, cann. 818–23.

[14] The grounds of nullity referring to conditioned consent can be found in the *Code of Canon Law*, cann. 1101–02; CCEO, cann. 824, 826.

[15] The grounds of nullity referring to defects of will can be found in the *Code of Canon Law*, cann. 1103, 1105 §4, 1106; CCEO, can. 825.

[16] *Code of Canon Law*, can. 1432; CCEO, can. 1096.

There are others also involved in the matter. A *canonical judge* is the person appointed to determine whether the marriage is invalid. Cases of marriage nullity generally require a court of three judges.[17] In certain circumstances, it is permissible for a bishop to allow a single judge to hear a case of marriage nullity. If only one judge is appointed on a marriage case, he must be a priest or deacon.[18] An *auditor* is a person appointed to assist the judge in gathering facts.[19]

A *procurator* is a person who acts in the name of one of the parties. An *advocate* is a person who defends the position of one of the parties. In most cases, a person using the services of a procurator or advocate must give permission for them to act. This permission is called a mandate.[20]

Procedures

There are four stages of the process itself. In the first stage, the petitioner requests the court to investigate the marriage and the case is accepted or rejected. Once accepted, the respondent becomes directly involved. In the second stage, the judge gathers the proofs. In the third stage, the proofs are revealed to all the parties involved. All have a right to know what information is being used to make a decision. If this right to know is denied, the procedural acts can be declared invalid and the process has to begin again. In the final stage, a decision is made and the parties are given the opportunity to appeal. Even if no appeal is made, a higher court must review and approve an affirmative decision before the parties are free to marry.[21]

While the petitioner must begin the process, the respondent and the defender of the bond have the same rights during the process as the petitioner. If the court acts properly, four natural rights are recognized and protected: the right to defense, the right to know the grounds, the right to know the judgment, and

---

[17] Cf. *Code of Canon Law*, can. 1425 §§1, 2; CCEO, can. 1084 §§1, 2.
[18] Cf. *Code of Canon Law*, can. 1425 §4; CCEO, can. 1084 §3.
[19] Cf. *Code of Canon Law*, can. 1428.
[20] Cf. *Code of Canon Law*, can. 1484; CCEO, can. 1142.
[21] Specific procedural norms are found in the *Code of Canon Law*, book VII, and CCEO, titles XXIV–XXVI.

the right to appeal. Specific violations of these rights are grounds for an appeal and may invalidate the process. Because of the technicalities in the procedures, it is always helpful for the parties to retain an advocate to help explain the process and protect their rights.

No one has a right to receive a declaration of nullity, nor is the process an opportunity "to get even" for problems that occurred during common life. The Church is concerned with the truth about the marriage. If the procedures are followed properly, there is a better chance the truth will be made known. When made known, regardless of the decision, "the truth will make you free" (Jn. 8:32).

Questions for Reflection or Group Discussion

1. What is the difference between a divorce and a declaration of nullity? How would I respond to someone who says that "an annulment is merely a Catholic divorce"?

2. Read no. 1632 in the *Catechism of the Catholic Church*. God's plan for marriage from the beginning is that it be indissoluble— "What therefore God has joined together, let no man put asunder" (Mt. 19:6). What can I do to foster holy and intact Christian marriages?

3. The Church teaches that if a couple is validly married, the couple remains married even if the state says they are not, and even if the couple no longer wishes to be married. Why is this so? (Read Catechism, nos. 1639–40; 2382–86.)

Chapter 16

SHOULD I ATTEND?
DEALING WITH PROBLEMATIC WEDDINGS

Does the Catholic Church prohibit Catholics from attending weddings that the Church does not recognize? If a Catholic is invited to such a wedding and can attend, is it permissible for him to be in the wedding party?

The Catholic Church does not explicitly prohibit Catholics from attending weddings whose validity she does not recognize. There are certain moral principles, however, that should be considered before a Catholic decides how to proceed. Most importantly, Catholics must avoid any actions that cause scandal or encourage others to sin.

In today's society, many couples live together before marriage, and divorce and remarriage are common. In addition, many Catholics marry outside the Church. Couples in these situations commit the sins of fornication, or adultery. Because of these objectively sinful circumstances, Christians are often left in a quandary when they are invited to weddings the Church does not recognize, particularly when friends or relatives are involved. The way in which one prayerfully responds to these invitations must witness to the truths taught by Christ. Our actions must encourage and promote the salvation of all.

Salt of the Earth

Everything we do must encourage and provide for our salvation and the salvation of others. We must be in the world, but not of the world (cf. Jn. 17:15–19). In our dealings with others, we must be salt of the earth and witness to the truths of Christ and His Church (cf. Mt. 5:13). When we seek our salvation and the salvation of others, we fulfill the two great commandments: to love God with our whole heart, mind and soul, and to love our neighbor as ourselves for the love of God (cf. Mt. 22:37–40). We must take care, however, not to become "insipid salt." As our Lord says, "You are the salt of the earth; but if salt has lost its taste, how shall its saltness be restored? It is no longer good for anything except to be thrown out and trodden under foot by men. You are the light of the world. A city set on a hill cannot be hid. Nor do men light a lamp and put it under a bushel, but on a stand, and it gives light to all in the house. Let your light so shine before men, that they may see your good works and give glory to your Father who is in heaven" (Mt. 5:13–16).

Contagious Grace

In the Old Testament, not only were sinners considered unclean, but also coming into contact with a sinner made a person unclean. In Jesus' own day, the Pharisees had a number of human regulations that were designed to keep the observant Jews cordoned off from Gentiles, lest the faithful be contaminated.

Jesus took a different approach. He spent time with tax collectors, adulterers, and other sinners. He sent His apostles "into all the world" (Mk. 16:15). The mere touch of Jesus brought healing to the sinner, without Jesus being contaminated (cf. Lk. 6:19). Note that Jesus didn't simply "hang out" with the wrong people. He affirmed their dignity and value, but He also used such occasions to say, "[D]o not sin again" (Jn. 8:11).

In continuing the work of Christ, the Church, without compromising her own holiness, embraces sinners and cleanses them with her sacraments (cf. Catechism, no. 827). Following Jesus' example, we need to associate with fellow sinners, yet do so in a way that is ordered to their salvation and ours.

Guiding Principles

If we allow or participate in the sin of another, we share that sin and its consequences. As the Catechism teaches, "Sin is a personal act. Moreover, we have a responsibility for the sins committed by others when *we cooperate in them:*

—by participating directly and voluntarily in them;
—by ordering, advising, praising, or approving them;
—by not disclosing or not hindering them when we have
  an obligation to do so;
—by protecting evil-doers" (no. 1868, emphasis in origianl).

The Catechism also teaches,

Scandal is an attitude or behavior which leads another to do
evil. The person who gives scandal becomes his neighbor's
tempter. He damages virtue and integrity; he may even draw his
brother into spiritual death. Scandal is a grave offense if by deed
or omission another is deliberately led into a grave offense. . . .
Anyone who uses the power at his disposal in such a way that it
leads others to do wrong becomes guilty of scandal and responsible for the evil that he has directly or indirectly encouraged.
"Temptations to sin are sure to come; but woe to him by whom
they come!" [Lk. 17:1] (nos. 2284, 2287).

Fornication and adultery are grave violations of the sixth
commandment (cf. Catechism, nos. 2331–2400). Those who
persist in these sins endanger their salvation. Living together
before marriage typically implies fornication (cf. Catechism,
no. 2353). The subsequent marriage of the couple does not blot
out the sins they already committed, nor does the wedding itself
necessarily change their attitudes or habits toward chastity
and purity. Remarriage following divorce is an act of adultery,
regardless of whether the "spouses" are Catholic or not (cf. Mk.
10:10–12; Catechism, no. 2384). When a Catholic marries
outside the Church, the Church does not recognize the marriage, and the union is considered illicit.[1]

What's a Catholic to Do?
If a Catholic is asked to attend the wedding of a couple
whose marriage is not recognized by the Church, he should ask
himself: "What message will I send by my attendance? Will

---

[1] Cf. *Code of Canon Law* (Washington, D.C.: Canon Law Society of America, 1983),
can. 1108.

attending such a wedding encourage or hinder the salvation of others? What will not attending accomplish? If I go, will others consider my presence to be affirming of the sin? Will I commit scandal? How can I best witness to the truth?" A Catholic should not affirm fornication or adultery, nor should he give the appearance to others that he condones the acts. Such appearance can cause scandal. If his actions affirm or encourage the sin, he participates in the sin.

There is a real concern that if a person refuses to attend the wedding, a rift in friendship could occur. This division could hinder any witness to the truth, and this concern is especially serious if the wedding involves a close friend or family member. This concern alone must not hinder our witness (cf. Lk. 12:51–53), but it can guide our actions as we fulfill our obligation to bring others to Christ. It could be that not attending would destroy any possible chance to witness the truth to the persons involved, especially if no reason is given for not attending. It could also be that not attending, and giving reasons for the absence, will help the couple choose the way of Christ. If a Catholic chooses to attend, he will want to ensure that no one considers his presence to be an affirmation of the sin.

Jesus saw the woman at the well and the Samaritans of her town as ripe for the harvest. Had He not spent two days with them, they would not have received the words of life. While with the Samaritans, Jesus encouraged His apostles to open their eyes and see the opportunity to spread the truth (cf. Jn. 4:1–42). We too must recognize the opportunities for reaping the harvest of faith, and not quench the burning embers among the lukewarm (cf. Is. 42:3–4).

Sending the Right Message

These principles apply whether one is a member of the wedding party, is attending the wedding, or is simply attending the reception. Participating in the wedding party, however, is more visible and will generally be understood as an affirmation of the union. It would be very difficult for a member of the wedding party to attend without affirming the situation or at least giving the impression to others that he is doing so. All who attend the reception should consider that discussions about the couple and their life together will arise. This may be more difficult for some people to handle without affirming the couple's situation or bringing scandal to others. If one plans to attend the reception, one should consider what one will say about the couple's situation when the merriment begins and everyone is talking about how wonderful this "marriage" is.

Morally speaking, there are many factors to consider before we judge such participation to be scandalous. Some situations are more conducive to scandal than others. Before we can witness to the truth, people must be open to what we have to say. In the same way, before our actions cause scandal, people have to consider our actions worthy of notice. What is important to remember is that we must prayerfully consider the situation, our response, and the probable reaction of others to our response. Using the teachings explained in the Catechism, we should ask ourselves, "How can we avoid participating in their sin, yet encourage their salvation? How can we avoid scandal, yet encourage the salvation of others?"

It is wise for anyone in this situation to discuss the matter with a spiritual director or confessor before making a decision. Whatever one's decision may be, a Catholic should strive to give a clear and charitable witness to the faith. The Church does not teach whether we must or must not attend such a wedding. Christ does say we must witness to the truth in a charitable manner. If loved ones or friends go through with the wedding, a Catholic should look for opportunities to maintain contact and witness to the truth. Above all, our decisions and actions must promote the salvation of souls. In fostering the salvation of souls, the two great commandments are fulfilled.

Questions for Reflection or Group Discussion

1. Read Catechism, no. 2284. What is the sin of scandal? How does it apply to the decision to attend a wedding?

2. What factors would be relevant in considering whether to attend a wedding not recognized by the Church? What would be the advantages and disadvantages of attending?

3. The reason this is such a significant issue is that premarital cohabitation, fornication, and divorce and remarriage are increasingly common today. What can we do within our own sphere of influence to reverse this trend and promote the Sacrament of Marriage?

Chapter 17

THE COMPLETE BIBLE
WHY CATHOLICS HAVE SEVEN MORE BOOKS

Catholic Bibles have forty-six Old Testament books; Protestant Bibles have thirty-nine. Catholics sometimes refer to these seven books as the deuterocanon[1] (second canon), while Protestants refer to them as the apocrypha, a term often used pejoratively to describe non-canonical books. Protestants also have shorter versions of Daniel and Esther. Why are there these differences?

Catholic Bibles contain all the books that traditionally have been accepted by Christians since Jesus' time. Protestant Bibles contain all those books, except those rejected by the founders of Protestantism in the 1500s. The primary reason why Protestants rejected these biblical books was that they did not support Protestant doctrines. For example, 2 Maccabees supports prayer for the dead, which most Protestants do not accept.[2]

The term *canon* means rule or guideline, and in this context means which books belong in the Bible (and, by implication, which do not).

The Catholic Old Testament follows the Alexandrian canon of the Septuagint, the Old Testament which was translated into Greek around 250 B.C.[3] The early Protestants followed the

---

[1] The seven books are Tobit, Judith, Wisdom, Sirach (Ecclesiasticus), Baruch, and 1 and 2 Maccabees.

[2] For similar reasons, Martin Luther rejected the canonicity of the Letter of James in the New Testament. However, others included James in their Bibles. James is part of the New Testament deuterocanon, which also includes 2 and 3 John, 2 Peter, Jude, Hebrews, and Revelation. Protestants accept the New Testament deuterocanon, but not the Old Testament deuterocanon. See CUF's FAITH FACT entitled "What's in a Name?" which further explores the distinction between the protocanon, deutero-canon, and the apocrypha.

[3] The Septuagint is often abbreviated as LXX.

Palestinian canon of Scripture, which was not officially recognized by Jews until around A.D. 100.

Dueling Canons

Prior to Jesus' time, the Jews did not have a universal, sharply defined canon of Scripture. Some groups of Jews used only the first five books of the Old Testament (the Pentateuch); some used only the Palestinian canon (thirty-nine books); some used the Alexandrian canon (forty-six books); and some, like the Dead Sea community, used all these and more. The Palestinian and Alexandrian canons were more normative than the others, having wider acceptance among orthodox Jews.[4]

The apostles commissioned by Jesus, however, used the Septuagint (the Old Testament in Greek which contained the Alexandrian canon) most of the time, and thus must have accepted the Alexandrian canon. Eighty-six percent of Old Testament quotes in the Greek New Testament come directly from the Septuagint, and there are numerous other linguistic references as well. Acts 7 provides an interesting piece of evidence that justifies the apostolic use of the Septuagint. In Acts 7:14, Saint Stephen says that Jacob came to Joseph with seventy-five people. The Palestinian version of Genesis 46:27 says "seventy," while the Septuagint version says "seventy-five," the number Stephen actually used. Stephen clearly used the Septuagint.

In the mid-twentieth century, scholars studying the Dead Sea Scrolls discovered older Hebrew manuscripts that agree with the Septuagint rather than the Masoretic texts.[5] We also know from other ancient Christian documents, like the Didache and Pope Saint Clement's Letter to the Corinthians,

---

[4] The Palestinian canon is sometimes called "Masoretic" after the medieval rabbis, who were called "Masoretes."

[5] Catholic Bible translations make use of the oldest and most accurate manuscripts, regardless of language, whenever possible. It was not known until late in the twentieth century that the number "75" (which Stephen used in Acts 7:14) was older and more reliable, so your own Bible probably does not say "75" in Genesis 46:27. Future translators who take the new evidence into account will probably fix the discrepancy between Acts and Genesis.

that the apostles' successors not only used the Septuagint, but quote from all of the books in the Alexandrian canon as the authoritative Word of God.[6]

Where's the Table of Contents?

There is no divinely inspired "table of contents" for the Bible. Therefore, Christians need an authority, such as the infallible Church established by Christ, to discern which books are the divinely inspired ones. (Indeed, even if there were such a table of contents list, we would need an authority to tell us if the list itself were inspired.) Many Evangelical Protestant Bible scholars admit as much: "While we know that at the time of Jesus there were different canons of the Old Testament because the canonical process was not yet complete, the glorious truth is that God has invited humans to be partners in the putting together of Scripture. I think the implications are that you cannot have Scripture without the community of faith [in other words, the Church]. It's not just a private revelation. God gives us Scripture, but then the [Church], by God's guidance, has to choose what's in and what's out."[7]

Why did the Palestinian Jews of A.D. 100 reject the Septuagint? First, it was written in Greek, which, after the destruction of Jerusalem by Gentiles, seemed "un-Jewish" or even "anti-Jewish."[8] Second, Christians, following the lead of their apostolic leaders, widely used the Septuagint, especially in apologetics to the Jews; thus, non-Christian Jews wanted to deny the value of some of its books, such as the Book of Wisdom, which contains a prophecy of Christ's death (cf. Wis. 1:16, 2:12–14). In the words of the Protestant Septuagint scholar Sir Lancelot Brenton: "The veneration with which the

---

[6] The Didache is a first-century document that contains teachings of Christ's apostles.

[7] Dr. Peter Flint, an Evangelical Protestant theologian who earned his doctorate at the University of Notre Dame, as quoted in Kevin Miller, "The War of the Scrolls," *Christianity Today* 41, no. 12 (October 6, 1997): 38–45.

[8] Scholars now know, based on evidence from the Dead Sea Scrolls, that some of the deuterocanonical books previously existed in Hebrew. It is likely that many of the Jews of A.D. 100 did not know this.

Jews had treated this [Septuagint] (as it is shown in the case of [Jewish historians] Philo and Josephus), gave place to a very contrary feeling when they found how it could be used against them [i.e., in Christian apologetics]: hence they decried the [Septuagint] version, and sought to deprive it of any authority."[9]

Protestant Objections

What are the classic Protestant arguments against the seven deuterocanonical books? Their major objection is that the deuterocanonicals contain doctrines and practices, such as the doctrine of purgatory and praying for the dead, that are irreconcilable with authentic Scripture. This objection, of course, begs the question. If the deuterocanon is inspired Scripture, then those doctrines and practices are not opposed to Scripture but part of Scripture. Another objection is that the deuterocanonical books "contain nothing prophetic." This is clearly proved false by comparing Wisdom 1:16–2:1 and 2:12–24 to Matthew's Passion account, especially Matthew 27:40–43.

Many Protestants also argue that because neither Jesus nor His apostles quote the deuterocanonical books, they should be left out of the Bible. But neither Jesus nor His apostles quote Ecclesiastes, Esther, or the Song of Songs, nor even mention them in the New Testament—yet Protestants accept these books. Further, the New Testament quotes and refers to many non-canonical books, such as the pagan poetry quoted by Paul (Acts 17:28) and Jewish stories referred to by Jude (Jude 9). Clearly, the quotation of a book in the New Testament, or the lack thereof, cannot be a reliable indicator of Old Testament canonicity.

Others argue that many Jews throughout history—particularly first-century Jews—have not accepted the deuterocanon. But why should Christians accept the authority of late first-century non-Christians instead of the example of the apostles? Would God found a Church upon the apostles (cf. 1 Cor. 3) and then let them fall into grave error about the Old Testament canon?

---

[9] Sir Lancelot C. L. Brenton, introduction to *The Septuagint with Apocrypha* (Grand Rapids: Zondervan Publishing House, 1980), iv.

Still others point to Saint Jerome's purported rejection of deuterocanonical material. While Jerome was initially suspicious of the "extra" Old Testament books, which he only knew in Greek, he fully accepted the judgment of the Church on the matter, as shown in a letter written in 402: "What sin have I committed in *following the judgment of the churches? . . .* I explained not what I thought [when I wrote the objections of the Jews to the longer form of Daniel in my introduction], but what [the Jews] commonly say *against us* [Christians who accept the longer form of Daniel]."[10]

Other Protestants claim that the Church did not authoritatively define the canon of Scripture until the Council of Trent and, since that council was a reaction to the Reformation, the deuterocanon can be considered an "addition" to the original Christian canon. This is also incorrect. Regional councils of the early Church had enumerated the books of the Bible time and again prior to the Reformation, always upholding the current Catholic canon.[11] Examples include Pope Saint Damasus (382), the Council of Hippo (393), and the Third and Fourth Councils of Carthage (397, 418), Pope Innocent (407), and the Council of Florence (1442).[12] *All of these affirmed the Catholic canon as we know it today*, while none affirmed the Protestant canon.

---

[10] Saint Jerome, *Jerome's Apology against Rufinus*, bk. 2, no. 33, in *Nicene and Post-Nicene Fathers*, 2nd ser., vol 3, eds. Philip Schaff and Henry Wace (Peabody, Mass.: Hendrickson Publishers, 1994), 517, emphasis added. Remember that Protestants reject the longer, Alexandrian version of Daniel; Saint Jerome did not. In addition, the Latin Vulgate version of the Bible, which Saint Jerome finished around A.D. 406 at the request of the pope, included the deuterocanonical books.

[11] Some will cite the writings of Saint Melito, bishop of Sardis, who wrote in the late second century, and Saint Athanasius, bishop of Alexandria, in the mid-fourth century. Both saints affirmed the Old Testament canon as best they knew it, and did exclude several deuterocanonical books. However, Melito included Wisdom, and Athanasius included Baruch while omitting all of Esther; so neither affirmed the Protestant canon. See William J. Jurgens, *The Faith of the Early Fathers*, vol. 1 (Collegeville, Minn.: Liturgical Press, 1970), 81 (no. 190), and 341–42 (no. 791).

[12] R. C. Fuller, "The Old Testament Canon," in *A New Catholic Commentary on Holy Scripture*, eds. Reginald Fuller, Leonard Johnston, and Conleth Kearns (Nashville, Tenn.: Thomas Nelson Publishers, 1975), 26.

Fallible Collection?

The Catholic canon also had the support of important Church Fathers like Saint Augustine.[13] A thousand years later, while seeking reunion with the Copts, the Church affirmed the same canon at the Ecumenical Council of Florence in 1442.[14] When the canon became a serious issue following the Protestant Reformation in the early 1500s, the Council of Trent dogmatically defined in 1546 what the Church had consistently taught.

R. C. Sproul, a prominent Protestant theologian, asserts that we must accept the Bible as a "fallible collection of infallible books,"[15] and many Protestants find this idea appealing. There are serious problems with this position, however. While it acknowledges that infallible books exist somewhere in the world, it implies that we can have no guarantee that all, or indeed any, of those infallible books are in the Bibles that Christians use. If the collection is fallible, the contents are not necessarily the books that are infallible. How do we know, then, that John's Gospel, which all Christians accept, is legitimately Scripture, while the so-called Gospel of Thomas, which most Christians reject, is not? Sproul's statement points to the need for an authority outside the Bible so that we can have an infallibly reliable collection of inspired books. It is ultimately contradictory to believe in the Bible's inspiration, and the reliability of its canon, without believing in the Church's infallibility.[16]

---

[13] Cf. Saint Augustine, *Christian Instruction* (397). This canon was, of course, supported by many more Church Fathers than the ones cited in this chapter, but these are examples of early Church Fathers who provide an exact list of the canonical books. Most Church Fathers took the canon for granted, quoting the Scriptures—including the deuterocanon—without formally listing them.

[14] The Council of Florence issued a binding decree on the subject; the Council of Trent affirmed Florence with its dogmatic definition.

[15] R. C. Sproul, *Essential Truths of the Christian Faith* (Wheaton, Ill.: Tyndale House, 1992), 22.

[16] In G. K. Chesterton's *The Catholic Church and Conversion* [(New York: Macmillan, 1926), 31–32], a humorous and rather convincing "man on the street" scenario illustrates the absurdity that an impartial bystander would see in denying the Church's infallibility while upholding the canon's inspiration as proclaimed by the Church.

To answer the question, "Who decided which books are in the Bible?" we must inevitably recognize the authoritative Church that Christ founded, the Church that infallibly discerned with God's guidance which books belonged and which did not. The longer Old Testament canon is the correct one.

Questions for Reflection or Group Discussion

1. How would I respond to a friend who says that "the Catholics have added seven books to the Bible"?

2. "Apocrypha" refers to texts that are not divinely inspired. Some apocryphal books may be very edifying and contain profound truths, but nonetheless are not divinely inspired and thus are not part of the Bible. Catholics maintain that the deuterocanonical books are truly part of the Bible and are not apocryphal. What difference does it make whether the deuterocanonical books are apocryphal? Have I read these books?

Recommendation: Use the index at the back of the Catechism to look up the references to these books and discover how the Church interprets them.

3. Protestants disagree with the Church about the deuterocanonical books. Aside from knowing more of the ecclesial, theological, and historical reasons for the Church's teaching, how can I respectfully and charitably address these issues with those from other religious traditions?

CALL NO MAN FATHER
UNDERSTANDING MATTHEW 23:9

Why do Catholics call priests "father," when Jesus says, "[C]all no man your father on earth" (Mt. 23:9)?

In Matthew 23:9, Jesus emphasizes the primary role of our heavenly Father. He created us in His image and likeness (cf. Gen. 1:26–28), and He made us His children through Baptism into the death and Resurrection of His Son (cf. Rom. 5:12–21; 6:3–4; 8:12–17). Because God created us in His image and likeness, we share in the attributes of God. Insofar as men share in the attributes of the Father, they participate in the one fatherhood of God.

In Matthew 23:9, Jesus says, "And call no man your father on earth, for you have one Father, who is in heaven." Many people interpret this to mean, "Do not call a priest 'father,' and do not call your dad 'father.'" Some who hold this opinion go farther and believe that calling a priest "father" violates Scripture because it seemingly involves the rejection of a direct command from Jesus. This is a fairly common objection to Catholic teaching.

But, if we believe the conclusion that it is wrong to call others "father," then what are we to make of the scriptural passages that contradict this one? For example, in Mark 7:9–13, Jesus criticizes the Pharisees and scribes for not honoring their "fathers." Furthermore, calling the apostles and their successors "father" was common within the early Christian communities (cf. Acts 7:2; 22:1; 1 Cor. 4:15; 1 Jn. 2:13–14). As in the case of all scriptural interpretations, we must understand this passage in light of the rest of Scripture (cf. 2 Pet. 1:20; 3:16). This interpretative principle is called the *analogy of faith* (cf. Catechism, no. 114).

Honor Thy Father

In the Old Testament, God commands: "Honor your father and your mother, as the LORD your God commanded you; that your days may be prolonged, and that it may go well with you, in the land which the LORD your God gives you" (Deut. 5:16). God gave this command after telling us to honor Him. With this in mind, it seems reasonable to conclude that God Himself considers others to be "fathers." Jesus upholds this commandment in Mark 7:9–13. In this passage, He berates the scribes and Pharisees, who used traditions to justify a failure to provide assistance to their fathers. Similarly, Jesus includes honoring one's human father as a prerequisite to attaining eternal life (cf. Mt. 19:16–19).

A father is one who begets children. Biologically, to beget means to give the seed from which a child is conceived. A man begets and a woman conceives. In the act of begetting, the man shares in the attributes of God's fatherhood by participating in the creation of this new life. In turn, God is the Author of life, Who actively creates a soul and infuses it into the child at the moment of conception.

It is important to remember that a child does not choose his biological father. The father gives the child life. Just as God gives life to all men, and so deserves our honor and reverence, so a child owes his life to his father, and the father deserves honor from the child.

There is a spiritual sense to fatherhood as well. Jesus identifies spiritual fatherhood in terms of whom one honors. If we honor the father of lies, the devil is our father; if we honor God, He is our Father (cf. Jn. 8:44–49). Thus, Jesus calls the devil the father of some, and He calls God the Father of others. Those who are alive in Christ owe their new life to God, but those who are in bondage to sin owe their enslaved existence to Satan. This passage allows us to understand better what Jesus meant in Matthew 23:9.

Text and Context

Matthew 23:9 is part of a larger passage in which Jesus comments on the example of the scribes and Pharisees. Saint Matthew devotes the entire chapter to this discourse. While reading the entire chapter is most helpful in understanding this passage, the first twelve verses provide adequate context to begin the discussion:

> Then said Jesus to the crowds and to his disciples, "The scribes and the Pharisees sit on Moses' seat; so practice and observe whatever they tell you, but not what they do; for they preach, but do not practice. They bind heavy burdens, hard to bear, and lay them on men's shoulders; but they themselves will not move them with their finger. They do all their deeds to be seen by men; for they make their phylacteries broad and their fringes long, and they love the place of honor at feasts and the best seats in the synagogues, and salutations in the market places, and being called rabbi by men. But you are not to be called rabbi, for you have one teacher, and you are all brethren. And call no man your father on earth, for you have one Father, who is in heaven. Neither be called masters, for you have one master, the Christ. He who is greatest among you shall be your servant; whoever exalts himself will be humbled, and whoever humbles himself will be exalted" (Mt. 23:1–12).

In the remainder of the chapter, Jesus expresses disgust with the many hypocrisies of the scribes and Pharisees. He ends by lamenting over Jerusalem for killing the prophets and ignoring the Word of God.

In Matthew 23, then, Jesus identifies two authorities, explains the proper response to authority in general, and condemns acts of pride and selfishness committed by those in authority. In doing all these things, He prepares the crowd for the New Covenant ratified by His Blood.

Who's Who?

Jesus notes that "[t]he scribes and the Pharisees sit on Moses' seat" (Mt. 23:2). By this, He recognizes that they have an obligation to teach the people as Moses taught the people. Because he received the Law from God and then gave it to the people, Moses was the mediator of the Old Covenant. The scribes and Pharisees cannot add to what Moses did, but only teach it. As teachers of this Law, they must be respected. This first authority was given by God through the Old Covenant, as expressed in the Mosaic Law. As successors of Moses, the scribes and Pharisees claimed this authority.

"Now the man Moses was very meek, more than all men that were on the face of the earth" (Num. 12:3). And when Miriam and Aaron spoke in pride, saying, "Has the LORD indeed spoken only through Moses? Has he not spoken through us also?" (Num. 12:2), God punished them (cf. Num. 12:9–16).

Unlike Moses, from whom they claim authority, the scribes and Pharisees used their positions for their own profit and glory. While Jesus tells the people, then, to follow the teachings of the scribes and Pharisees, He warns them not to follow their prideful practices. As God punished Miriam and Aaron for their pride, so Jesus warns the scribes and Pharisees of punishment for theirs. One such act of pride was to be called teacher, father, and master. As in other places of Scripture, Jesus emphasizes here that one who seeks to be a teacher, father, or master must serve the rest, and not seek one's own glory or power. He also introduces a second authority, which would be rooted in the New Covenant ratified in His Blood. This authority is rooted in service to the People of God, a service ordered to the sanctification of all men. As only the successors of Moses could claim the authority under the Mosaic Law, only the successors of Jesus—the apostles and their successors—can claim this authority today.

Jesus identifies fatherhood with His Father in heaven, and authority with the authority He received from His Father (cf. Mt. 23:9–10). In a different way, He made the same identification in Matthew 10:40. In that passage, Jesus commissioned His twelve apostles and sent them out in His name. Jesus told them, "He who receives you receives me, and he who receives me receives him who sent me." In this way, the apostles knew they acted not on their own authority, but on the authority of Jesus Christ, the Son of God. Furthermore, those who accepted them were accepting Christ and His Father in heaven (cf. Mt. 18:5; Mk. 9:37; Lk. 9:48; Jn. 12:44; 13:20; Gal. 4:14).

Our father is the one whose authority we choose to honor. In Matthew 23:9, Jesus exhorts us to choose His Father and those who act in His name.

Priests of the New Covenant

At the Last Supper, Jesus gave His Church the gift of the ministerial priesthood and reconfirmed the authority He had given to the apostles. He gave His apostles the authority to act in His person with the authority given Him by the Father. Jesus had already given them this authority, as noted in Matthew 10:40, and He reemphasized it in John 17 when, while praying to the Father, He said, "While I was with them, I kept them in thy name, which thou hast given me. . . . As thou didst send me into the world, so I have sent them into the world" (Jn. 17:12, 18). Those who share in this authority make present the graces necessary for our spiritual rebirth and sustenance in Christ. For it is through the apostles' successors—the bishops and the priests who share in this ministry—that the precious Body and Blood of our Lord become present and our sins are absolved.

The title "father" does not confer upon priests the same honor due to our heavenly Father alone, nor does it diminish God's absolute and universal fatherhood. However, it is incorrect to interpret Matthew 23:9 in an exclusively literalistic sense. Saint Paul, inspired by the Holy Spirit, writes, "For though you have countless guides in Christ, you do not have many fathers. For I became your father in Christ Jesus through the gospel" (1 Cor. 4:15). Saint Paul calls himself "father" because he recognizes his cooperation with God in begetting the spiritual life of the community entrusted to his care. There are several other passages which show that the title "father" was applied to others in the New Testament besides God and biological fathers (cf. Acts 7:2; 22:1; 1 Cor. 4:15; Philem. 10; 1 Jn. 2:13–14).

Where Do We Go from Here?

We cannot interpret Matthew 23:9 as prohibiting reference to biological fathers or priests as "fathers" without contradicting other scriptural passages in which the word "father" is used. Such an interpretation would render the commandment "Honor your father" meaningless and would diminish the authority of the apostles and their successors. Admittedly, it is easier for a Protestant to accept the title "father" for those who beget children biologically. To use the title for others might imply the recognition of Jesus' intention to establish apostolic spiritual fatherhood in the Church.

However, our lives of faith are conceived by the acts of those who sow the seeds of faith. The apostles and their successors were commissioned by Christ Himself. They bear His Word in our lives and are ministers of His grace through the sacraments of the Church, beginning with our spiritual rebirth in Baptism. By sharing in the high priesthood of Christ, bishops and priests share in the attributes of the Father. As there is no father but the one Father in heaven, and no teacher or master but Christ, we properly understand that these men, having been commissioned by Christ to act in His Person, also represent the Father, Whom the Son reveals (cf. Jn. 1:14–18), and uniquely participate in the spiritual begetting of God's children. Saint Ignatius of Antioch, who knew the apostles, expressed this well when he wrote: "Let everyone revere . . . the bishop as the image of the Father [*Ad Trall.* 3, 1: SCh 10, 96]" (Catechism, no. 1554).

When discussing this issue with others who do not agree with us, it is helpful to refer them to the passages mentioned above and to ask them for an explanation of the meanings. Remind those with whom we are discussing this topic that God cannot contradict Himself, so the Scriptures, which are His Word, cannot be contradictory. After hearing their answers, charitably question any contradictions.

Most importantly, find common ground through which you can further an understanding of fatherhood. This common ground will probably be at the level of biological fatherhood. On this level, interpreting Matthew 23:9 in an exclusively literal sense would undermine the Fourth Commandment. Most will recognize that in no way does this title take away from the ultimate power and authority God has over human life: "[T]hou didst knit me together in my mother's womb" (Ps. 139:13). Rather, we recognize that all fatherhood comes from God, as Saint Paul teaches: "For this reason I bow my knees before the Father, from whom every family in heaven and on earth is named. . . ." (Eph. 3:14–15, Douay Rheims Version).

In this context, we can explain the fatherhood of bishops and priests. Rather than bearing merely human authority and following the example of pride set by the scribes and Pharisees, bishops and priests bear the authority of God in the New Covenant, sealed with the Blood of Christ. With such a commission, bishops and priests are called to live in service to others.

Thus, whether we are speaking of biological fathers or spiritual fathers, we understand men in both circumstances to be participating in the one fatherhood of God. Human fatherhood is a gift from God and must be lived in a godly manner. Only in this way can human fathers—biological and spiritual—raise their children to be children of light.

Questions for Reflection or Group Discussion

1. What does my human father teach me about God's fatherhood? How does God's fatherhood surpass that of my human father?

2. Do I recognize bishops and priests as truly being fathers? How do I understand their fatherhood?

3. How would I explain to a friend or colleague that calling a priest "father" does not entail a rejection of Jesus' command in Matthew 23:9? What role, if any, would the fourth commandment ("Honor thy father and mother") play in my explanation? What other biblical passages are relevant to the discussion?

Chapter 19

AN ORDINANCE FOREVER
THE BIBLICAL ORIGINS OF THE MASS

What are the biblical origins of the Mass and the New Testament priesthood? Is the Mass really a sacrifice, or is it merely symbolic?

The biblical origins of the Mass and the New Testament priesthood are rooted in the Old Testament. Both the Old and New Testaments provide clear evidence that the Mass is a true sacrifice, offered by a priest, and the Victim is the Body and Blood, Soul and Divinity of Jesus Christ.

God stated three times that the Passover sacrifice would be "an ordinance for ever," not for a temporary period, such as until the Messiah came. This sacrifice, and other Old Covenant sacrifices, find their culmination in Christ's sacrifice on Calvary (Ex. 12:14, 17, 24; cf. Lk. 22:7–20). Christ's sacrifice at the Last Supper was a sacrifice of His Body and Blood, Soul and Divinity (cf. Catechism, nos. 1362–67, 1373–77). Much as the sacrifice offered at the Last Supper fulfilled the Old Covenant sacrifices, the priesthood of Christ—the priesthood of Melchizedek—replaced the Levitical priesthood of the Old Testament. This New Testament priesthood, handed on to the apostles and their successors, allows Christ's sacrifice on Calvary to fulfill the perpetual ordinance of a sacrifice through the celebration of the Mass (cf. Heb. 6:19–7:28).

Prefiguring the Lamb of God
God made a covenant with Abraham, swearing that all the nations (Gentiles) would bless themselves through his descendants (cf. Gen. 22:18). He designated Mount Moriah as the place where He would provide the sacrificial lamb, which was prefigured by the lamb that Abraham sacrificed that day (cf. Gen. 22:4–14). God the Father fulfilled the sacrificial provision in an ultimate way by offering His only-begotten Son (cf. Gen. 22:2; Jn. 3:16), the Lamb of God (cf. Rev. 5:6).

Interestingly, Mount Moriah's location, Salem, is another name for Zion or Jerusalem (cf. 2 Chron. 3:1; Ps. 76:2). In fact, Scripture identifies Mount Moriah as the site of Solomon's Temple in Jerusalem, the city in which Christ's sacrificial death took place. Also, Melchizedek was the priest and king of Salem (cf. Gen. 14:18). Jesus, as the Lamb of God Who takes away the sin of the world, is the definitive High Priest according to the order of Melchizedek; Jesus offers Himself as the sacrifice of salvation and the universal blessing through whom all the nations will bless themselves (cf. Gen. 22:18; Acts 3:17–26; Heb. 6:19–7:28).

According to the terms of the Old Covenant, the Passover sacrifice has to be offered at the Temple in Jerusalem (cf. Deut. 16:1–6; 2 Chron. 35:1–19), a sacrifice that has not occurred since the Temple's destruction in A.D. 70. One is left with two alternatives. First, one could state that Israel has failed to keep the covenant with God recorded in Exodus 12. Yet if that is true, God is thereby implicated for failing to provide His People with the means to continue the ordinance that He told them to keep forever.

Alternatively, one could state that the Temple sacrifice was destined by God to become obsolete and that, as the Lamb of God, Jesus perfectly fulfilled the Passover sacrifice (cf. 1 Cor. 5:7). This is the teaching of the Church. Jesus prophesied the fall of the Temple (cf. Mt. 24:1–2), an event that happened in A.D. 70 shortly after the "desolating sacrilege" of the Temple (Mt. 24:15). In addition, while prophets accurately foretold that the Temple would be rebuilt after its destruction in 587 B.C., no subsequent biblical prophets prophesied the Temple's restoration after Christ's predicted destruction.

Attempts to rebuild the Temple have failed, most notably the effort of the Roman Emperor Julian the Apostate in 362. He hoped to discredit Christ's prophecy about the Temple. When violent earthquakes at the site killed many of his workmen, Julian abandoned his attempt.[1]

---

[1] Cf. George Sim Johnston, "Notes from the Apocalypse Watch," *Lay Witness* 15, no. 11 (September 1994): 4–5.

The question remains: How does the Passover sacrifice of Jesus Christ continue as an ordinance forever? Just as the old Passover lamb freed the People of the Old Covenant from the bondage of slavery, the new Passover Lamb frees us from the slavery of sin (cf. Mt. 26:28). In accepting Saint John the Baptist's designation of Jesus as the new Lamb of God (Jn. 1:29–35), Jesus states clearly that He will be both sacrificed and eaten (cf. Lk. 22:7–20; Jn. 6:51–66), just as the old Passover lamb was both sacrificed and eaten (cf. Ex. 12:8–11). Unfortunately, most contemporary Protestants do not accept this biblically based teaching about the Real Presence of Christ in the Eucharist.[2]

Transcending Time and Space

The quick Protestant rejoinder to Catholic teaching on the Mass is that Christ died "once for all" (cf. Heb. 9:26–28; 10:10), to which the Church would say, "Amen!" The Church has always taught that the one sacrifice of Christ and the sacrifice of the Eucharist (the Mass) are "*one single sacrifice*," and that the Eucharistic Sacrifice "*re-presents* (makes present)" Christ's sacrifice on the Cross (Catechism, nos. 1366–67, emphasis in original). How can this be? God the Son created time and space and, therefore, is not bound by them (cf. Jn. 1:1–3). As eternal Being, Christ stands outside of time, and therefore, all of history is simultaneously present to Him. We cannot fully grasp God's omnipotence. Like the dogmas of the Trinity or Christ's being both God and man, God's omnipotence is beyond our capacity to understand, yet does not contradict reason. To argue that God is limited by time and space is necessarily to argue that God is not omnipotent, and therefore not God.

In short, then, God cannot create something, including time and space, that can limit Him. For example, because of God's omnipotence, all of us, not just one of us, can be temples of the Holy Spirit (cf. 1 Cor. 6:19). This demonstrates His abil-

---

[2] Interestingly, Martin Luther and John Calvin, leaders of the Protestant Reformation, believed in the Real Presence, although their doctrine was inaccurate. Luther believed that Christ's Body and Blood were present with the bread and wine, while Calvin believed Christ was present spiritually with the bread and wine. Neither, however, recognized the sacrificial nature of the Mass.

ity to be beyond space, for the Holy Spirit is present in the souls of all believers: the saints who have died (cf. Rev. 6:9–11), as well as all the faithful who are living today.

We can also speak of God's ability to be present throughout time on earth and also outside of time in heaven. Relative to God, Who is eternal and unchanging, everything is present; relative to us human beings, everything we experience is bound by time and space. Because the Son of God is eternal and transcends time, what He does as the God-Man in history can transcend time. Jesus' sacrifice on Calvary is thus once for all, yet never ending; it is timeless. Thus, when we re-present Christ's one sacrifice at Mass, God actually enables us to make ourselves present to this timeless offering. Analogously, we become "present" to the sun each morning. The sun basically stays put, while we change relative to the sun because of the earth's daily rotation.

The Eucharistic sacrifice is foreshadowed by the prophet Malachi: "For from the rising of the sun to its setting my name is great among the nations, and in every place incense is offered to my name, and a pure offering; for my name is great among the nations, says the LORD of hosts" (Mal. 1:11). The Church sees these verses as a prophecy of the Sacrifice of the Mass, for what other truly pure sacrifice could there be that Christians can offer throughout the world every day?

The Mass's transhistorical nature is first illustrated when Christ offered His glorified Body and Blood at the Last Supper, the day before He actually died on the Cross (cf. Catechism, nos. 1337–40). It is illustrated thereafter in the Mass offered by His disciples. Saint Paul notes that Christ's sacrifice as the new Passover Lamb is once for all, but he also explains that its celebration somehow continues on in history: "For Christ, our paschal lamb, has been sacrificed. Let us, therefore, celebrate the festival, not with the old leaven, the leaven of malice and evil, but with the unleavened bread of sincerity and truth" (1 Cor. 5:7–8). Thus, the merits of Christ's sacrifice are applied to Christians throughout the centuries.

We speak of the Eucharist as an unbloody sacrifice. Christ is not killed at each Mass. If that were so, there would be many sacrifices, and Christ would not have died "once for all." Rather, the Council of Trent teaches that at each Mass "the same Christ who offered himself once in a bloody manner on the altar of the cross is contained and offered in an unbloody manner [*Doctrina de ss. Missae Sacrificio*, c. 2: DS 1743; cf. Heb. 9:14, 27]" (Catechism, no. 1367).

He's Got His Whole Self . . . in His Hands?

Some people ask incredulously, "Could God hold Himself in His hands at the Last Supper? And how could He offer up a sacrifice the day before He actually died?" The short answer is that Jesus could because He can do all things (cf. Mt. 19:26), such as when He appeared to His disciples in the flesh miraculously after His Resurrection, despite locked doors. To answer these questions about the Last Supper adequately, we must examine the biblical and other historical evidence for the sacrificial nature of the Eucharist by analyzing whether God really offered His Body and Blood, Soul and Divinity at the Last Supper, and whether priests re-present the same sacrifice at every Mass.

Consider Jesus' words: "[H]e who eats my flesh and drinks my blood has eternal life, and I will raise him up at the last day. For my flesh is food indeed, and my blood is drink indeed. He who eats my flesh and drinks my blood abides in me, and I in him. . . . [H]e who eats this bread will live for ever" (Jn. 6:54–56, 58).

Some Christians argue that Christ meant this statement figuratively, just as He did when He described Himself as the "vine" or the "door" (Jn. 10:7–9; 15:1–5). However, "to eat the body and drink the blood" of someone was an ancient Hebrew idiom that meant to slander a person. The Old Testament testifies to this figurative meaning: "When evildoers assail me, uttering slanders against me, my adversaries and foes, they shall stumble and fall" (Ps. 27:2). A footnote in the Revised Standard Version Catholic Edition confirms that "uttering slanders against me" in Hebrew literally means "to eat up my flesh." If we then insert the figurative meaning in John 6:54, Jesus says that "he who slanders me has eternal life." Such a figurative interpretation would make our divine Lord look very foolish.

While the Levitical priesthood prohibited the consumption of blood (cf. Lev. 17:10–14; see also Gen. 9:1–4), Jesus came to do away with and yet fulfill this temporary discipline. Given that this Levitical prohibition and similar ones that were still in force when Christ preached on the Eucharist in Capernaum, one could understand the Jews' disbelief and would, therefore, expect Christ to clarify Himself if He intended a figurative interpretation of His words. However, despite the ensuing departure of many of His followers (cf. Jn. 6:66), Jesus did not back down from His command to eat His Body and drink His Blood.

Like the Passover lambs before Him, Jesus would be both sacrificed and eaten. Whereas animal blood symbolized life and thus yielded imperfect atonement (cf. Lev. 17:11), Jesus freely offers us His Blood—indeed commands consumption (cf. Jn. 6:54–55)—because His Blood provides us redemptive life and perfect atonement.

Saint Paul affirms Christ's Real Presence during the sacrifice of the Mass (cf. 1 Cor. 11:23–32). How can people "be guilty of profaning the body and blood of the Lord" (1 Cor. 11:27), and why are they getting sick and even dying, if they are merely consuming bread and wine? As Jesus teaches and Saint Paul affirms, the re-presentation of this one offering—this "breaking of bread" (Acts 2:42)—was to continue in the Church. We partake of this one sacrifice in a sacramental manner, under the appearance of bread and wine, and in a way that does not diminish God, Who is infinite. Jesus not only fulfills Passover in Easter, but also makes it possible for the New Covenant of His sacrifice to be re-presented every day at Mass.

The Priesthood of Melchizedek

Christ's priesthood forever according to Melchizedek (cf. Ps. 110:4; Heb. 5:6) makes clear the connection between the Last Supper, Jesus' Crucifixion, and the Mass. When Christ died on Calvary, "he became the source of eternal salvation to all who obey him, being designated by God a high priest after the order of Melchizedek" (Heb. 5:9–10). While Christ suffered and died once for all, His sacrifice on Calvary is somehow connected with, and continues forever according to, a Melchizedekian offering or sacrifice: one using the elements of bread and wine (cf. Gen. 14:17–20). On the day before He died on the Cross, Jesus "pre-presented" and anticipated His completed, glorified sacrifice under the appearances of bread and wine (cf. Lk. 22:19–20) and thus manifested that He is not constrained by time (cf. Catechism, nos. 1337–40). Fulfilling Christ's command to "[d]o this in remembrance of me" (Lk. 22:19), the Church re-presents this same timeless offering of His Body and Blood under the appearances of bread and wine.

Indeed, as a faithful Priest Who continues to intercede for His People in Heaven after His death and Resurrection, Jesus must have something to offer. He does, and it can only be His one, definitive, and never-ending sacrifice (cf. Rev. 5:1–14), which He continues to offer forever as a priest according to the order of Melchizedek through His priests on earth (cf. Catechism, no. 1337). While Jesus does not need to re-present His sacrifice sacramentally to save us, He faithfully continues the Passover ordinance forever as His gift to us, reminding us daily of His great love and providing us with abundant graces to aid our journey to heaven. "When the Church celebrates the Eucharist, she commemorates Christ's Passover, and it is made present: the sacrifice Christ offered once for all on the cross remains ever present [cf. Heb. 7: 25–27]. 'As often as the sacrifice of the Cross by which 'Christ our Pasch has been sacrificed' is celebrated on the altar, the work of our redemption is carried out' [LG 3; cf. 1 Cor. 5:7]" (Catechism, no. 1364).

Christ is the one mediator between God and man (cf. 1 Tim. 2:5), but He allows certain men to participate in His mediation, by exercising authority in general (cf. Mt. 28:18–20), granting forgiveness of sin (cf. Jn. 20:21–23), and re-presenting His one sacrifice sacramentally (cf. Mt. 26:26–28). The Catholic Church is the new Israel, a spiritual house, and a holy priesthood (cf. 1 Pet. 2:5). The Eucharist is disconcerting to some Christians, not only because it simultaneously shows God's awesome omnipotence and humble condescension, but also because it reminds us that salvation is not a momentary, once and for all event, but a process that involves our saying yes to God each and every day. Salvation is by grace, but our free assent is needed for the gift of salvation to be efficacious in our lives.

Christ has perfected the Passover ordinance. He has torn down the barrier between God and man, enabling us to be reconciled to the Father and partake again of His divine nature (cf. Rom. 5:15–17; 2 Pet. 1:4). Heeding Christ's command, we continue re-presenting and partaking of His sacrifice at every Mass. While this is a "hard saying" (Jn. 6:60), it is very much in keeping with salvation history, and not too remarkable for a God Who created us out of nothing and became man to save us from our sins. Our response to such an incredible gift should echo the words of Saint Peter, when Christ asked him if he also would leave Him: "Lord, to whom shall we go? You have the words of eternal life; and we have believed, and have come to know, that you are the Holy One of God" (Jn. 6:68–69).

Questions for Reflection
or Group Discussion

1. How is Jesus Christ the new and definitive Passover Lamb?

2. How would I respond to the objection that Christ died "once for all" (Heb. 9:26), yet Catholics offer this sacrifice over and over again? See Catechism, nos. 1366–67.

3. How does my understanding of the sacrificial nature of the Mass affect my attitude toward the Eucharist? See Romans 12:1–2 and Colossians 1:24. What can I do to offer my own life in union with Christ crucified?

Chapter 20

A SIGN OF THE TIMES?
UNDERSTANDING THE ENNEAGRAM

What is the Enneagram? May Catholics use the Enneagram?

The Enneagram is a symbol that is designed geometrically. The symbol is made up of nine lines of equal length connecting to form a nine-pointed star. A circle connecting the nine points completes the Enneagram symbol (see diagram, p. 153).

Because it is merely a symbol that is designed geometrically, the Enneagram itself presents no offense to faith or morals. However, the use of the Enneagram for cultic or pseudoscientific practices can pose a threat to Catholic belief and practices. For this reason, in 2003, two pontifical councils advised that the Enneagram "when used as a means of spiritual growth introduces an ambiguity in the doctrine and life of the Christian faith."[1]

The Enneagram as a Symbol

"In human life, signs and symbols occupy an important place. As a being at once body and spirit, man expresses and perceives spiritual realities through physical signs and symbols. As a social being, man needs signs and symbols to communicate with others, through language, gestures, and actions. The same holds true for his relationship with God" (Catechism, no. 1146).

Given the beauty and goodness of the natural world (cf. Gen. 1:31), man commonly uses various creatures or combines characteristics of different creatures to symbolize certain things. Because these natural symbols are limited, different cultures and peoples commonly use the same symbol, but attribute to it different meanings. For example, the rainbow is a symbol used by almost every culture in every time of humanity.

---

[1] Pontifical Council for Culture and Pontifical Council for Interreligious Dialogue, *Jesus Christ: The Bearer of the Water of Life* (February 3, 2003), 1.4; available from www.vatican.va.

Christians commonly use the rainbow as a symbol of God's promises and a hope for the future. It is common to see the rainbow combined with the Cross to show the fulfillment of God's promises in the death and Resurrection of Christ.

Various sects, however, also see significance in the colors of the rainbow.[2] The meanings they attribute to the rainbow certainly have nothing to do with the fulfillment of God's promises. Other symbols used differently by various peoples are the sun, moon, and stars.

Man also creates new symbols from natural shapes and designs. For example, the Star of David is a shape made up of six lines of equal length connected in such way as to form a six-pointed star. The pentagram is a star made from five lines of equal length connected to form a five-pointed star. Both stars are used as symbols by various cultures to mean different things. The Enneagram is simply a nine-pointed star made up of nine lines of equal length and having a circle connecting its points.

Modern Uses of the Enneagram

Of itself, no symbol is evil. However, the meanings and uses of the symbol can be evil. Thus, the issue is whether the symbol, as it is understood by a particular culture, represents something good and beneficial, or evil and harmful.

The Enneagram has existed for hundreds and possibly thousands of years. While its date of origin is disputed, it came to the United States in the 1960s, at which time it was developed into a pseudo-scientific system for analyzing personality.[3] The diagram was discovered in the 1890s in Central Asia by the Greek-Armenian occultist George Gurdjieff. He received it from the Sufis, who were using it for numerological fortune-telling. Oscar Ichazo, a follower of Gurdjieff, added animal sym-

---

[2] Robert Emmet Long, ed., *Religious Cults in America*, vol. 66, no. 4 (New York: H. W. Wilson, 1994), 79.

[3] Father Mitch Pacwa, S.J., an expert on occult and New Age issues, affirms that the Enneagram's use as a personality tool dates back to the 1960s and thus dispels the myth that its use for this purpose dates back to antiquity. For an excellent overview of the theological and pastoral difficulties associated with the Enneagram, see Mitch Pacwa, S.J., *Catholics and the New Age* (Ann Arbor, Mich.: Servant Publications, 1992), 111–24.

bols, or totems, and attributed certain personality types to the various points on the star. Psychologist Claudio Naranjo used the diagram as a tool for evaluating personality types. His students subsequently disseminated this use throughout the world.[4]

Today, the Enneagram is still related to the occult and is also used in the United States as a tool of personality evaluation. Some people merge both uses. Proponents of the New Age movement and certain occult groups believe that the Enneagram symbolizes the nine faces of God, which become nine demons when turned upside down. This dualism is not compatible with Christianity. It is also used in rituals of channeling spirits, horoscopes, meditations, drug use, and rituals of channeling spirits. Some attribute certain esoteric powers of self-salvation to the use of the Enneagram. These Gnostic and Pelagian ideas are in direct contradiction to the truths of the Catholic faith.[5]

Within the psychological disciplines, the Enneagram is often used as a tool of personality evaluation. Each of the nine points on the star represents a personality type. Each personality type has a vice and virtue connected with it. The various lines connecting the points inside the diagram and the circle connecting the points outside the diagram represent the various relationships that exist between personality types. These lines also are used to project methods of personality development and growth.

In 2000, Father J. Augustine Di Noia, O.P., Executive Director of the Secretariat for Doctrine and Pastoral Practices of the United States Conference of Catholic Bishops, and now Undersecretary of the Congregation for the Doctrine of the Faith, issued a report on the Enneagram, which concludes as follows: "[T]hose who are looking for an aid for personal and psychological development should be aware that Enneagram teaching lacks a scientific foundation for its assertion and that the Enneagram is of questionable value as a scientific tool for

---

[4] Cf. Mitch Pacwa, S.J., "Tell Me Who I Am, O Enneagram," *Christian Research Institute Journal* (Fall 1991), 14; available from www.equip.org/free/DN067.htm.

Cf. U.S. Bishops' Secretariat for Doctrine and Pastoral Practices, *A Brief Report on the Origins of the Enneagram*; available from www.natcath.com.

[5] Cf. Mitch Pacwa, S.J., "Is the Enneagram Dangerous?" *New Covenant* 21, no. 1 (July/August 1991), 20–24.

the understanding of human psychology. Moreover, Christians who are looking for an aid for spiritual growth should be aware that the Enneagram has its origins in a non-Christian world-view and remains connected to a complex of philosophical and religious ideas that do not accord with Christian belief."[6]

The reliability and validity of the Enneagram system of per-sonality evaluation have not been demonstrated scientifically. Many psychologists will recommend its use, but their recom-mendations are based purely on personal opinion, not objective criteria. All personality evaluation tools are limited in their reliability. Because the Enneagram lacks objective testing, its limitations are more pronounced. As such, those who attempt to "baptize" the Enneagram should take to heart Saint Paul's wise admonition to "test everything; hold fast to what is good, [and] abstain from every form of evil" (1 Thess. 5:21–22).

Can the Enneagram Be "Baptized"?

"God created everything for man [cf. GS 12 § 1; 24 § 3; 39 § 1], but man in turn was created to serve and love God and to offer all creation back to him" (Catechism, no. 358). Consequently, our use of signs and symbols must be useful for sal-vation. Any contrary use is not an act of love and service of God.

Unfortunately, some Catholics use the Enneagram in the manner described earlier in this chapter. Such use of the Enneagram does not contribute to catechetical and spiritual formation. Use of the Enneagram as a personality evaluation tool is also touted as definitive and reliable, even though this is not the case.

If the Enneagram is to be used as a thing of beauty and move people to salvation, the occult, Pelagian, Gnostic, and pseudo-scientific uses that have been associated with the Enneagram must be avoided. Pure Catholic meanings would have to be attributed to it for it to have value within the Church. For example, as an object of art, it could bear much beauty, just as other geometric designs bear much beauty. As a symbol, the circle could symbolize the eternity of God and the nine points could symbolize His absolute perfection (three times three).

---

[6] Secretariat for Doctrine and Pastoral Practices, *A Brief Report on the Origins of the Enneagram*.

Any proper Christian meanings attributed to the Enneagram would have to be known to all who see it. If such a common understanding is not established, the meaning is useless. As Catholics, we must avoid the use of the symbol entirely, or attribute to it purely Catholic meanings.

_____*SideBar*___

Enneagram Diagram

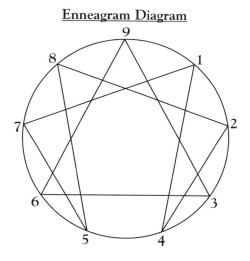

Questions for Reflection
or Group Discussion

1. What are some of the symbols that are associated with the Christian faith? Are these symbols susceptible to other meanings if used by other cultures?

2. Some people have tried to adapt the Enneagram to help Christians better understand themselves. Why is this a worthwhile objective? Why can't the Enneagram, in light of its history, help Christians to meet this objective?

3. How would you explain to someone your reasons for not using the Enneagram? How would you apply 1 Thessalonians 5:21–22 in discussing the Enneagram?

Chapter 21

LET THE SON SHINE
THE TRUTH ABOUT THE NEW AGE MOVEMENT

May Catholics participate in New Age activities?

No. The ideas associated with the New Age movement are incompatible with the Catholic faith. They are incompatible with doctrines essential to Christianity, such as the Trinity, the divinity of Christ, the redemptive sacrifice of Christ on Calvary, and the God-ordained necessity of the Church for salvation. The New Age movement is rooted in the ideology and practice of witchcraft. Because of the direct opposition between New Age ideas and the truths of the faith, participation in New Age activities is gravely sinful and is offensive to Christ and His Church.

The New Age movement is characterized by a combination of practices and beliefs. Those who promote doctrines of the New Age movement root their ideas and practices in theosophic philosophy, the occult, pantheism, and many teachings of non-Christian, Eastern religions. Many of these ideas have spread among Catholics and other Christians. As our Holy Father points out, there are many who are "unaware of the incompatibility of those ideas with the Church's faith."[1]

Origin and Early Development

Theosophist philosophy provides the modern foundation of the New Age movement. One of the founders of the Theosophical Society was Helena Petrovna Blavatsky, who published *Isis Unveiled* in 1877.[2] This book contains information about primitive scientific practices, Eastern philosophy,

[1] Pope John Paul II, *Address to U.S. Bishops* (May 28, 1993).
[2] Cf. Theosophical Society in America; available from http://www.theosophical.org/society/intro/index.html.

witchcraft, and even serpent worship. Her fascination with the occult developed after she met the diabolic "master" of her dreams. The Theosophical Society's periodical, *Lucifer*, was published to spread its beliefs throughout the world.[3]

In 1891, Petrovna was succeeded as president of the Theosophical Society by Annie Wood Besant. Besant wrote under the pen name "Ajax." Within her writings, she promoted ideas such as the necessity of birth control.[4]

Four of the basic ideas of the Theosophical Society—later embraced by the New Age movement—can be summarized as follows:

1. The constitution of the soul is pantheistic.
2. The evolution of man to a higher consciousness enables him to achieve perfection.
3. The reincarnation of the soul benefits man as he inches closer towards perfection.
4. The force of one's activities (karma) determines one's reincarnated state.

Under the pontificate of Benedict XV, the Holy See condemned theosophic doctrines. The Holy Office, when asked "[w]hether the doctrines which are called theosophic can be reconciled with Catholic doctrine," gave a negative reply.[5]

Thus the Holy See's condemnation encompasses more than the Theosophic Society itself: The condemnation extends to all theosophic doctrines and forbids joining any society that promotes theosophic doctrines, attending meetings of such societies, and reading any materials of these societies.

---

[3] Cf. Theosophical Society in America; available from http://www.theosophical.org/theosophy/questmagazine/septoct2001/algeo/.
[4] Cf. Annie Wood Besant, *The Law of Population: Its Consequences and Its Bearing Upon Human Conduct and Morals* (New York: A. K. Butts, 1878).
[5] Reply by the Holy Office dated July 18, 1919. Text found in *Canon Law Digest*, ed. T. Lincoln Bouscaren, S.J., vol. 1 (Milwaukee: The Bruce Publishing Company, 1934), 620.

Pantheism

Pantheism is a philosophy of religion that denies the Christian understanding of God as three divine Persons in one God. Pantheists believe that the entire natural order, both visible and invisible, makes up the being of "god." This god is considered to be a limited, always changing, impersonal force. Because everything is god, all gods are true gods and man himself is god. This error in the understanding of God is at the heart of all other errors.

New Age proponents express their pantheistic belief in various ways. Some divinize the created world in which we live. They believe the created order is actually a god personified, hold that a higher consciousness exists in all things, and believe that the purpose of life is to become aware of and enter into union with that higher consciousness. Some believe in Gaia, the mother goddess of all. Others worship Mother Earth. Still others worship Isis. In a twisting of Catholic doctrine, the liturgical honoring of Mother Earth takes place, and the Blessed Virgin is seen to be the goddess Isis. Some go so far as to identify the earth with Christ. Many believe the wounded earth will rise in the third millennium and usher in the dawn of a New Age and the destruction of the Catholic Church.[6]

In general, New Age philosophy promotes an understanding of creation contrary to the truths of the Catholic faith. The philosophy denies that God created all, that Christ redeemed man, and that man has dominion "over all the earth" (Gen. 1:26). The general philosophy emphasizes the existence of a common, psychic memory or consciousness found in all things. This common element unites us and embodies the reality of God. In violation of the First Commandment (cf. Ex. 20:3), this movement encourages the worship of false gods, particularly the worship of the earth and all creation.

Perfection through a Higher Consciousness

Proponents of the New Age movement often refer to a higher consciousness that enables man to achieve perfection or

---

[6] Mitch Pacwa, S.J., *Catholics and the New Age* (Ann Arbor, Mich.: Servant Publications, 1992), 184–185.

union with all. According to this mistaken belief, as man acquires a greater awareness of the common spirit in all things, he moves toward greater harmony and union with all. He achieves awareness through means like transcendental meditation. A common form of these means introduced into the Catholic Church is the technique of centering prayer.[7] Communication with this purported higher consciousness within all things is made through anagrams, horoscopes, and other techniques (cf. Catechism, no. 2116).

The belief in and desire for union with a higher consciousness leads to a mistaken belief that man can transcend the evils of the world through his own power. Because man himself is god (according to this view), he creates his own reality that transcends the pains and problems of the world. An immediate and dangerous error flowing from this is the belief that man does not need Christ. Evil and sin are seen as a consequence of a lack of awareness and union, not a free choice. New Age proponents believe that an individual no longer has his own conscience; rather, they believe that the conscience belongs to an accumulated whole. This belief attacks the notions of an individual soul and salvation by Christ.

We are saved by the grace of God received through the Church established by Christ (cf. Catechism, nos. 846–48). Our sins are forgiven because of Christ's death on the Cross (cf. Catechism, nos. 606–23). Alone, we could never hope to achieve Heaven and attain the beatific vision of our Creator. We are not saved by our own acts, nor do we achieve union with God through techniques of transcendental meditation and means of communication with a common spirit. As noted above, belief in a higher consciousness present in all things denies the hierarchical ordering of creation. Such belief raises man to the level of God and ultimately leads to a denial of the reality of sin, guilt, eternal punishment, and the salvation offered through Christ's death on the Cross.

---

[7] Centering prayer is an attempt to harmonize transcendental meditation and Catholic contemplative prayer. Cardinal Ratzinger has noted the dangers of some methods associated with centering prayer. *New Heaven/New Earth* published an article on this topic entitled "Centering Prayer Meets the Vatican." For a reprint copy, call CUF at (800) MY-FAITH (693-2484).

Reincarnation and Karma

Reincarnation is the belief in the rebirth of the soul after death, into a new body or form of life. According to some, if your life was good, you are reincarnated into a higher consciousness. If your life was bad, you are reincarnated into a lower consciousness.

The goodness or evil of each life is determined by karma. A Hindu term meaning "action" or "force," karma refers to a series of cause-and-effect events that affect the moral and physical order of the universe. Each soul inherits its own karma from a previous life after it has been reincarnated. Obtaining a good karma is central to obtaining good fortune in the next life.

Following the theosophists, the New Age movement adopted this philosophy of reincarnation and karma. Many associated with the New Age movement regard this entire process as a method of growth and maturity through evolution. Despite the underlying pantheism of the belief system, some erroneously find these beliefs compatible with Christianity. In short, they adopt religious syncretism—the belief that all religions are essentially the same. They deny that the Catholic Church, or any other community, has the right to declare itself as the possessor of the true religion.

"Mello" Out

The information offered above is only an introduction to the errors of the New Age movement. In general, its doctrines and philosophies contradict the truths of the faith. The movement denies the nature of the triune God—Father, Son, and Holy Spirit. It denies the divine and human natures of Christ, His unique role as Messiah, and the necessity of His death for the salvation of all. It distorts the nature of man and denies that the ultimate purpose of man is union with God in Heaven.

New Age philosophy contains many contradictions and tolerates acceptance of conflicting beliefs. Such an approach allows practically anyone who holds to New Age ideas to claim allegiance to a particular religion. This approach readily encourages nominal Christians to be formed in New Age beliefs but still consider themselves members of their particular religion. Unfortunately, some Catholics ascribe to and participate in New Age activities. Some use the writings of Fathers Pierre Teilhard de Chardin, S.J., and Anthony de Mello, S.J., to prove compatibility of these beliefs with the Catholic faith. Indeed, both priests promoted ideas and beliefs that the New Age movement embraces.[8]

In considering the published works of Father de Chardin, the Holy Office stated, "Without undertaking to pass judgment on matters which pertain to the positive sciences, it is sufficiently clear that in the field of philosophy and theology the said works contain such ambiguities and even such grave errors as to offend against Catholic doctrine."[9] The statement concludes with a warning that his writings should not be used lest people be led astray.

The Congregation for the Doctrine of the Faith also noted serious errors in the writings of Father de Mello. Among errors found in his writings are the following assertions:

—A profession of faith and belief in God or in Christ impedes access to truth.
—The Catholic Church has made the Sacred Scriptures into an idol and banished God from the Temple.
—The Catholic Church has lost its authority to teach in the name of Christ.
—Evil is mere ignorance.
—There is no objective rule of morality.
—Good and evil are mere mental evaluations imposed on reality.

Consequently, the congregation stated that his writings are "incompatible with the Catholic faith and can cause grave harm."[10]

---

[8] Randy England, *The Unicorn in the Sanctuary: The Impact of the New Age on the Catholic Church* (Rockford, Ill.: Tan Books, 1992), 78–95, 101–104.
[9] *Monitum* issued by the Holy Office (June 30, 1962). Text found in *Canon Law Digest*, T. Lincoln Bouscaren, S.J., and James I. O'Connor, S.J., eds., vol. 5 (Milwaukee: The Bruce Publishing Company, 1963), 621–22.
[10] "Notification Concerning the Writings of F. Anthony de Mello, S.J.," *L'Osservatore Romano*, n. 34 (August 26, 1998), 5–6.

In Deuteronomy, God warns: "There shall not be found among you . . . any one who practices divination" (Deut. 18:10). Also forbidden is collaborating with "a soothsayer, or an augur, or a sorcerer, or a charmer, or a medium, or a wizard, or a necromancer. For whoever does these things is an abomination to the LORD; and because of these abominable practices the LORD your God is driving them out before you. You shall be blameless before the LORD your God" (Deut. 18:10–13).

As noted above, the Church has forbidden embracing theosophic philosophies and practices. Because the New Age movement is a theosophic movement, participation in the movement is an act of disobedience to the Church.

Most Catholics who participate in the New Age movement lack proper formation in the Catholic faith. Their lack of formation allows the lies and pitfalls of theosophic philosophies to go unnoticed. Such Catholics should be brought to a deeper understanding of the faith through catechesis.

To foster effective dialogue with these Catholics, we need three things:

1. **Proper formation.** We must be properly formed in the faith. We cannot explain the faith if we do not know it and live it. By living the faith, we invite others to seek the truth.

2. **Strong prayer life.** At the heart of discipleship is a strong prayer life. Through prayer, we come to know God intimately, and receive grace to soften the hearts of those to whom we witness.

3. **Understanding, patience, and charity.** We must under stand that we do not change people. God provides the grace, and we can offer an opportunity, but the ultimate decision belongs to the person involved. To be most effective in providing an opportunity, we must try to understand why a person believes what he believes. If we understand his reasons for participating in the New Age movement, we can better refute the errors. Through patience we can better understand the person, and through charity we can better witness to the truth.

In our witness to the truth, we must not lose heart, but strengthen our efforts through fellowship, the sacraments, and prayer. We must remain close to the Magisterium and heed the guidance of our sacred pastors.[11] Most importantly, we must keep the great commandments: to love God above all things, with our whole heart, mind, and soul, and to love our neighbor as ourselves for the love of God (cf. Mt. 22:34–40). These laws find their greatest fulfillment in the salvation of souls, wherein the angels in heaven rejoice (cf. Lk. 15:7).

Questions for Reflection
or Group Discussion

1. What is the history of the Theosophical Society? What has been the Church's response to this movement?

2. Read Catechism, nos. 2110–28. Why do New Age beliefs and practices involve a violation of the First Commandment?

3. Do I know anyone who is currently involved in the New Age movement? How can I effectively evangelize or catechize such individuals?

---

[11] For the most recent statements of the Church on the New Age, see Pontifical Council for Culture and Pontifical Council for Interreligious Dialogue, *Jesus Christ: The Bearer of the Water of Life: A Christian Reflection on the "New Age"* (February 3, 2003); available from www.vatican.va.

WHERE TWO OR THREE ARE GATHERED
SMALL FAITH COMMUNITIES

Should small faith communities be encouraged as a means of strengthening or renewing families, parishes, and dioceses?

Small faith or ecclesial base communities can be a great asset to families, parishes, and dioceses if they are faithful in teaching and living authentic Catholic doctrine. In fact, local chapters of Catholics United for the Faith are structured in a small group format. Problems have occurred in other small faith communities when they have taught Catholic doctrine inaccurately or vaguely, sometimes substituting personal experience for objective truth.

In the years following the Church's emergence or manifestation to the world on Pentecost (cf. Catechism, no. 1076), some communities of Christians were small. As Saint Luke tells us, "they devoted themselves to the apostles' teaching and fellowship, to the breaking of bread and the prayers" (Acts 2:42). The first "small faith communities," which later came to be known as parishes, existed to live and spread the authentic Catholic faith, which was received from the apostles. They were of one mind in faithfully and joyfully living out the call to follow Christ (cf. Acts 2:42–48).

Catholic Extension

In addition to parishes, many forms of small faith communities are flourishing in the Church today. They often emerge because people want to live out their faith with greater fervor through a more intimate system of support than the larger parish community is often able to provide. They may seek to learn Catholic doctrine, read and study the Scriptures, and deepen fraternal charity. They can be particularly helpful in cities where life is often impersonal, or in areas which lack the clergy necessary to form a parish community. They should, however, exist with the purpose of actually drawing the community together in union with the parish's pastor. In this sense, these communities are helpful for the individual person as well as a great service to the Church. Pope Paul VI has outlined the positive and proper role of small faith communities:

> These . . . communities will be a place of evangelization, for the benefit of the bigger communities, especially the individual Churches. . . . they will be a hope for the universal Church to the extent:
>
> —that they seek their nourishment in the Word of God and do not allow themselves to be ensnared by political polarization or fashionable ideologies, which are ready to exploit their immense human potential;
> —that they avoid the ever present temptation of systematic protest and a hypercritical attitude, under the pretext of authenticity and a spirit of collaboration;
> —that they remain firmly attached to the local Church in which they are inserted, and to the universal Church, thus avoiding the very real danger of becoming isolated within themselves, then of believing themselves to be the only authentic Church of Christ, and hence of condemning the other ecclesial communities;
> —that they maintain a sincere communion with the pastors whom the Lord gives to His Church, and with the magisterium which the Spirit of Christ has entrusted to these pastors;
> —that they never look on themselves as the sole beneficiaries or sole agents of evangelization—or even the only depositaries of the Gospel—but, being aware that the Church is much more vast and diversified, accept the fact that this Church becomes incarnate in other ways than through themselves;
> —that they constantly grow in missionary consciousness, fervor, commitment and zeal;
> —that they show themselves to be universal in all things and never sectarian.

"On these conditions, which are certainly demanding but also uplifting," the Pope continues, "the ecclesial base communities will correspond to their most fundamental vocation: as hearers of the Gospel which is proclaimed to them and privileged beneficiaries of evangelization, they will soon become proclaimers of the Gospel themselves."[1]

Lay Missionaries

In this age of the laity, where laypeople are encouraged to take their place in the "new evangelization," there is an ever-increasing need for lay people to work together in small faith communities to build up the Catholic Church. These small faith communities are recognized as lay apostolates that cooperate with bishops and priests within dioceses and parishes to further the mission of the Church.

> Since, like all the faithful, lay Christians are entrusted by God with the apostolate by virtue of their Baptism and Confirmation, they have the right and duty, individually or grouped in associations, to work so that the divine message of salvation may be known and accepted by all men throughout the earth. This duty is the more pressing when it is only through them that men can hear the Gospel and know Christ. *Their activity in ecclesial communities is so necessary that, for the most part, the apostolate of the pastors cannot be fully effective without it* [cf. LG 33] (Catechism, no. 900, emphasis added).

In his 1988 apostolic exhortation *Christifidelis Laici*, Pope John Paul II, drawing heavily upon the rich teaching of the Second Vatican Council on the laity, sets forth clear, definite criteria for determining whether an association of lay faithful is in keeping with the Church's communion and mission. These criteria are:

---

[1] Pope Paul VI, Apostolic Exhortation on Evangelization in the Modern World *Evangelii Nuntiandi* (December 8, 1975), no. 58.

—*The primacy given to the call of every Christian to holiness*, as it is manifested "in the fruits of grace which the spirit produces in the faithful" and in a growth towards the fullness of Christian life and the perfection of charity. In this sense whatever association of the lay faithful there might be, it is always called to be more of an instrument leading to holiness in the Church, through fostering and promoting "a more intimate unity between the everyday life of its members and their faith."

—*The responsibility of professing the Catholic faith*, embracing and proclaiming the truth about Christ, the Church and humanity, in obedience to the Church's Magisterium, as the Church interprets it. For this reason every association of the lay faithful must be a *forum* where the faith is proclaimed as well as taught in its total content.

—*The witness to a strong and authentic communion* in filial relationship to the Pope, in total adherence to the belief that he is the perpetual and visible center of unity of the universal Church, and with the local Bishop, "the visible principle and foundation of unity" in the particular Church, and in "mutual esteem for all forms of the Church's apostolate." The communion with Pope and Bishop must be expressed in loyal readiness to embrace the doctrinal teachings and pastoral initiatives of both Pope and Bishop. Moreover, Church communion demands both an acknowledgment of a legitimate plurality of forms in the associations of the lay faithful in the Church and at the same time, a willingness to cooperate in working together.

—*Conformity to and participation in the Church's apostolic goals*, that is, "the evangelization and sanctification of humanity and the Christian formation of people's conscience, so as to enable them to infuse the spirit of the gospel into the various communities and spheres of life."

—*A commitment to a presence in human society*, which in light of the Church's social doctrine, places it at the service of the total dignity of the person.[2]

---

[2] Pope John Paul II, Post-Synodal Apostolic Exhortation on the Vocation and the Mission of the Lay Faithful in the Church and in the World *Christifideles Laici* (December 30, 1988), no. 30, emphasis in original, citations omitted.

A House Divided

Regrettably, some groups that call themselves "small faith communities" are characterized by a spirit of bitterness and criticism directed against Church authority. They set themselves up as independent structures and attempt to undermine the established order.

Many difficulties can arise when small faith communities are not committed to the teachings of the Church. These difficulties include: replacement of the Church's hierarchical structure with self-appointed local teachers; the alteration of Church teaching, making it more conformable with the views of the community; and the governance of the parish by the small faith community rather than by Christ acting through the visible hierarchy. Instead of leading men and women to Christ, such communities set themselves up as an alternative to the hierarchy of the Church.

Small faith communities have a responsibility for the evangelization of their members that will lead beyond the group, to their parish, and out into the world. They are effective as long as they remain connected to the larger Church communities (their parish and diocese), rather than attempting to replace them in authority. In this way, they positively contribute to the growth and development of the Church throughout the world.

Particularly through its chapter program, Catholics United for the Faith supports small faith communities and encourages a healthy prudence in their activities, in keeping with the teaching of the Second Vatican Council and recent popes on the authentic role and mission of the laity.

Questions for Reflection
or Group Discussion

1. Am I currently involved in any lay organizations or small faith communities? Do they meet the criteria set forth by Pope John Paul II for assessing lay associations?

2. Why do some small faith communities go astray? Read John 15:1–11, and Catechism, no. 862. What dangers arise when a community sets itself in opposition to the pope or the local Church?

3. What can I do, both by individual endeavors and by working with other Catholics, to make Christ better known and loved in my community?

Recommended References

General

Aquilina, Mike. *The Fathers of the Church: An Introduction to the First Christian Teachers.* Huntington, Ind.: Our Sunday Visitor, 1999.

Catechism of the Catholic Church. 2nd ed. United States Catholic Conference, Inc.—Libreria Editrice Vaticana, 1994. *Modifications from the Editio Typica,* 1997.

Code of Canon Law, Latin-English Edition. Washington: Canon Law Society of America, 1983.

Flannery, Rev. Austin, O.P., *Vatican II: The Conciliar and Post Conciliar Documents.* Vols. 1 and 2. Northport, N.Y: Costello Publishing Co., 1996.

Hahn, Scott and Leon J. Suprenant, Jr., eds. *Catholic for a Reason: Scripture and the Mystery of the Family of God.* Steubenville, Ohio: Emmaus Road, 1998.

Hahn, Scott. *First Comes Love: Finding your Family in the Church and the Trinity.* New York: Doubleday, 2002.

Ignatius Bible. Revised Standard Version Catholic Edition. San Francisco: Ignatius Press.

Ignatius Catholic Study Bible. With introduction, commentary, and notes by Scott Hahn and Curtis Mitch. San Francisco: Ignatius Press.

Jurgens, William A., ed. *The Faith of the Early Fathers.* 3 vols. Collegeville, Minn.: The Liturgical Press, 1970–79.

The Navarre Bible. Dublin: Four Corners Press.

Ott, Ludwig. *Fundamentals of Catholic Dogma.* Trans. Patrick Lynch. Saint Louis: Herder, 1960. Reprint, Rockford, Ill.: TAN Books & Publishers, 1974.

Servants of the Gospel: Essays by American Bishops on Their Role as Shepherds of the Church. Steubenville, Ohio: Emmaus Road, 2000.

Stravinskas, Rev. Peter M. J. *A Tour of the Catechism.* Libertytown, Ill.: Marytown Press, 1996.

Suprenant, Leon J., Jr. and Philip C. L. Gray. FAITH FACTS: *Answers to Catholic Questions.* Vol. 1. Steubenville, Ohio: Emmaus Road, 1999.

Suprenant, Leon J., Jr., ed., *Catholic for a Reason II: Scripture and the Mystery of the Mother of God.* Steubenville, Ohio: Emmaus Road, 2000.

Tobin, Most Rev. Thomas J. *Without a Doubt: Bringing the Faith to Life.* (Steubenville, Ohio: Emmaus Road, 2001.

CREED

Denzinger, Henry. *Sources of Catholic Dogma.* Loreto Publications, 1954.

Hahn, Scott. *Hail, Holy Queen: The Mother of God in the Word of God.* New York: Doubleday, 2001.

Keating, Karl. *What Catholics Really Believe—Setting the Record Straight: 52 Answers to Common Misconceptions about the Catholic Faith.* San Francisco: Ignatius Press, 1992.

Kreeft, Peter. *Everything You Wanted to Know about Heaven.* San Francisco: Ignatius Press, 1990.

Kreeft, Peter, ed. *Summa of the Summa.* San Francisco: Ignatius Press, 1990.

Mangan, Rev. Charles. *Walking with the Pilgrim Pope.* Queenship Publishing, 1997.

Martin, Regis. *What Is the Church? Confessions of a Cradle Catholic.* Steubenville, Ohio: 2003.

McBride, Rev. Alfred, O.Praem. *Essentials of the Faith.* Updated ed. Huntington, Ind.: Our Sunday Visitor, 2002.

Meagher, James L. *How Christ Said the First Mass.* New York: Christian Press Association, 1906. Reprint, Rockford, Ill.: TAN Books & Publishers, 1984.

Morse, George, ed. *Précis of Official Catholic Teaching on the Church.* Silver Springs, Md.: Catholics Committed to Support the Pope.

Morse, George, ed. *Précis of Official Catholic Teaching on Christ Our Lord, True God and True Man.* Silver Springs, Md.: Catholics Committed to Support the Pope.

Most, Rev. William G. *The Consciousness of Christ.* Front Royal, Va.: Christendom Press, 1980.

Schönborn, Christoph Cardinal. *From Death to Life: The*

Christian Journey. San Francisco: Ignatius Press, 1995.

Sertillanges, Rev. A. G., O.P. *What Christ Saw From the Cross.* Manchester, N.H.: Sophia Institute Press, 1996.

Sheed, Frank. *Theology and Sanity.* San Francisco: Ignatius Press, 1993.

<u>LITURGY</u>

Budnik, Mary Ann. *Looking for Peace? Try Confession.* RB Media.

Daily Roman Missal. Huntington, Ind.: Our Sunday Visitor, 1998.

Documents on the Liturgy 1963-1979: Conciliar, Papal, and Curial Texts. Collegeville, Minn.: Liturgical Press, 1982.

Elliott, Msgr. Peter J. *Ceremonies of the Modern Roman Rite.* San Francisco: Ignatius Press, 1995.

Gaudoin-Parker, Michael. *Real Presence through the Ages: Jesus Adored in the Sacrament of the Altar.* Staten Island: Alba House, 1993.

General Instruction of the Roman Missal. United States Catholic Conference, 2003.

Gray, Tim. *Sacraments in Scripture: Salvation History Made Present.* Steubenville, Ohio: Emmaus Road, 2001.

Groeschel, Rev. Benedict J., C.F.R., and James Monti. *In the Presence of Our Lord.* Huntington, Ind.: Our Sunday Visitor, 1997.

Hahn, Scott. *The Lamb's Supper: The Mass as Heaven on Earth.* New York: Doubleday, 1999.

Handbook of Prayers. Princeton, N.J.: Scepter Press, 1992.

Hahn, Scott. *Lord Have Mercy: The Healing Power of Confession.* New York: Doubleday, 2003.

Instruction from various dicasteries of the Holy See. *Instruction on Certain Questions Concerning the Collaboration of the Lay Faithful in the Ministry of Priests.* August 15, 1997.

Pope John Paul II. On the Eucharist and Its Relationship to the Church *Ecclesia de Eucharistia.* April 17, 2003.

Likoudis, James and Kenneth Whitehead. *The Pope, the Council, and the Mass: Answers to the Questions the "Traditionalists" Are Asking.* W. Hanover, Mass.: Christopher Publishing House, 1981.

Morse, George P. *The Mass: Its Mysteries Revealed.* Catholics
Committed to Support the Pope.
Morse, George, ed. *Précis of Official Catholic Teaching on
Worship and the Sacraments.* Silver Springs, Md.: Catholics
Committed to Support the Pope.
Pope Paul VI. Encyclical of the Holy Eucharist *Mysterium
Fidei.* September 3, 1965.
Vatican II Sunday Missal and *Vatican II Weekday Missal.*
Pauline Books and Media.

CHRISTIAN LIVING
Cavins, Jeff and Matthew Pinto. *Amazing Grace for Those
Who Suffer.* West Chester, Pa.: Ascension Press, 2002.
Cessario, Rev. Romanus O.P. *The Moral Virtues and
Theological Ethics.* South Bend, Ind.: University of Notre
Dame Press, 1991.
Chervin, Ronda. *Living in Love: About Christian Ethics.*
Boston: St. Paul Books and Media, 1988.
DeMarco, Donald. *The Many Faces of Virtue.* Steubenville,
Ohio: Emmaus Road, 2000.
Eusebius. *Ecclesiastical History.* Peabody, Mass.: Hendrickson,
1998.
Gabriel, Stephen. *Speaking to the Heart: A Father's Guide to
Growth in Virtue.* Huntington, Ind.: Our Sunday Visitor,
1999.
Gray, Tim and Curtis Martin. *Boys to Men: The Transforming
Power of Virtue.* Steubenville, Ohio: Emmaus Road, 2001.
Hardon, Rev. John A., S.J., *The Question and Answer
Catholic Catechism.* Doubleday, 1981.
Lewis, C. S. *The Four Loves.* New York: Harcourt, Brace, 1960.
Martin, Michaelann. *Woman of Grace: A Bible Study for
Married Women.* Steubenville, Ohio: Emmaus Road, 2000.
Matthews, Elizabeth. *Precious Treasure: The Story of Patrick.*
Steubenville, Ohio: Emmaus Road, 2002.
Mitch, Stacy. *Courageous Love: A Bible Study on Holiness for
Women.* Steubenville, Ohio: Emmaus Road, 1999.
Morse, George, ed. *Précis of Official Catholic Teaching on the
Christian Call to Personal Sanctification.* Silver Springs,
Md.: Catholics Committed to Support the Pope.

Morse, George, ed. *Précis of Official Catholic Teaching on the Social Teaching of the Church*. Silver Springs, Md.: Catholics Committed to Support the Pope.

Pacwa, Rev. Mitch. *Father Forgive Me for I Am Frustrated*. Ann Arbor, Mich.: Charis, 1996.

Pieper, Josef. *On Hope*. Trans. Mary Frances McCarthy. San Francisco: Ignatius Press, 1968.

Pieper, Josef . *The Four Cardinal Virtues: Prudence, Justice, Fortitude, Temperance*. Notre Dame, Ind.: University of Notre Dame Press, 1966.

Pope Paul VI. Encyclical of the Regulation of Birth *Humanae Vitae*. July 25, 1968.

Pope John Paul II. *Letter to Families*. February 2, 1994.

Pope John Paul II. Apostolic Letter at the Close of the Great Jubilee of the Year 2000 *Novo Millennio Ineunte*. February 2, 1994.

Pope John Paul II. On the Vocation and the Mission of the Lay Faithful in the Church and in the World *Christifideles Laici*. December 30, 1988.

Pope John Paul II. On the Most Holy Rosary *Rosarium Virginis Mariae*. October 16, 2002.

Saint Francis de Sales. *Thy Will Be Done*. Manchester, N.H.: Sophia Institute Press, 1995.

HUMAN LIFE ISSUES

Drogin, Elasah. *Margaret Sanger: Father of Modern Society*. New Hope, Ky.: CUL Publications, 1989.

Grisez, Germain. *The Way of the Lord Jesus*. Vols. I, II, III. Chicago: Franciscan Herald Press, 1996.

Kasun, Jacqueline. *The War Against Population: The Economics and Ideology of World Population Control*. San Francisco: Ignatius Press, 1988.

Lee, Patrick. *Abortion & Unborn Human Life*. Washington: Catholic University of America Press, 1996.

Morse, George, ed. *Précis of Official Catholic Teaching on the Sanctity of Human Life*. Silver Springs, Md.: Catholics Committed to Support the Pope.

National Conference of Catholic Bishops. *Ethical and Religious Directives for Catholic Health Facilities*. Washington: United States Catholic Conference, 1975.

O'Donnell, Thomas, S.J. *Medicine and Christian Morality: Second Revised and Updated Edition*. Staten Island: Alba House, 1991.

Pope John Paul II. Encyclical On the Value and Inviolability of Human Life *Evangelium Vitae*. March 25, 1995.

Pope John Paul II. Encyclical for the Twentieth Anniversary of "Populorum Progressio" *Sollicitudo Rei Socialis*. December 30, 1997.

Pope Paul VI. Encyclical on the Development of Peoples *Populorum Progressio*. March 26, 1967.

MARRIAGE AND FAMILY LIFE ISSUES

Marks. Frederick W. *A Catholic Handbook for Engaged and Newly Married Couples*. Steubenville, Ohio: Emmaus Road, 2001.

Martin, Michaelann and Curtis. *Family Matters: A Bible Study on Marriage and Family*. Steubenville, Ohio: Emmaus Road, 2002.

Morse, George, ed. *Précis of Official Catholic Teaching Marriage, Family and Sexuality*. Silver Springs, Md.: Catholics Committed to Support the Pope.

Pope Paul VI. Encyclical of the Regulation of Birth *Humanae Vitae*. July 25, 1968.

Pope John Paul II. *Letter to Families*. February 2, 1994.

Pope John Paul II. Encyclical Regarding Certain Fundamental Questions of the Church's Moral Teaching *Veritatis Splendor*. August 6, 1993.

Pope John Paul II. On the Role of the Christian Family in the Modern World *Familiaris Consortio*. November 22, 1981.

Second Vatican Council. Pastoral Constitution on the Church in the Modern World *Gaudium et Spes*. December 7, 1965.

Stebbins, H. Lyman. *The Priesthood of the Laity in the Domestic Church*. Catholics United for the Faith.

Von Hildebrand, Alice. *By Love Refined: Letters to a Young Bride*. Manchester, N. H.: Sophia Institute Press, 1989.

Wilson, Mercedes Arzu. *Love and Family: Raising a Traditional Family in a Secular World*. San Francisco: Ignatius Press, 1996.

BIBLICAL APOLOGETICS
Butler, Scott, Norman Dahlgren, and David Hess. *Jesus, Peter, & the Keys: A Scriptural Handbook on the Papacy*. Santa Barbara, Calif.: Queenship Publishing, 1996.

Cavins, Jeff. *My Life on the Rock: A Rebel Returns to His Faith*. Ascension Press, 2002.

Currie, David. *Born Fundamentalist, Born Again Catholic*. San Francisco: Ignatius Press, 1996.

Danielou, Jean Cardinal, S.J., *The Bible and the Liturgy*. Notre Dame, Ind.: University of Notre Dame Press, 1956.

Graham, Henry. *Where We Got the Bible: Our Debt to the Catholic Church*. Catholic Answers, 1994.

Gray, Tim. *Mission of the Messiah: On the Gospel of Luke*. Steubenville, Ohio: Emmaus Road, 1998.

Hahn, Scott. *A Father Who Keeps His Promises*. Ann Arbor, Mich.: Charis, 1998.

Keating, Karl. *Catholicism and Fundamentalism*. San Francisco: Ignatius Press, 1988.

Kellmeyer, Steve. *Scriptural Catholicism*. Greyden Press.

Madrid, Patrick. *Pope Fiction: Answers to 30 Myths and Misconceptions about the Papacy*. Basilica Press, 1999.

Madrid, Patrick. *Surprised by Truth*. Vol. 1. Basilica Press, 1994.

Madrid, Patrick. *Surprised by Truth*. Vols. 2 and 3. Manchester, N.H.: Sophia Institute Press.

McBride, Rev. Alfred. *Essentials of the Faith*. Updated ed. Huntington, Ind.: Our Sunday Visitor, 2002.

Morrissey, Gerard. *Defending the Papacy*. Front Royal, Va.: Christendom Press, 1984.

Pope John Paul II. On the Vocation and the Mission of the Lay Faithful in the Church and in the World *Christifideles Laici*. December 30, 1988.

Ray, Stephen K. *Crossing the Tiber: Evangelical Protestants Discover the Historical Church*. San Francisco: Ignatius Press, 1997.

Shaw, Russell. *Papal Primacy in the Third Millennium*. Huntington, Ind.: Our Sunday Visitor, 2000.

Shea, Mark P. *By What Authority? An Evangelical Discovers Catholic Tradition*. Huntington, Ind.: Our Sunday Visitor, 1996.

Sri, Edward P. *Mystery of the Kingdom: On the Gospel of Matthew*. Steubenville, Ohio: Emmaus Road, 1999.

Stravinskas, Rev. Peter. *The Bible and the Mass: Understanding the Scriptural Basis of the Liturgy*. Ann Arbor, Mich.: Servant Publications, 1989.

Stravinskas, Rev. Peter. *The Catholic Church and the Bible*. San Francisco: Ignatius Press.

Stravinskas, Rev. Peter. *Tour of the Catholic Catechism*. Libertyville, Ill.: Marytown Press, 1992.

Vanhoye, Albert. *Old Testament Priests and the New Priest*. Trans. Bernard Orchard. Petersham, Mass.: Saint Bede's Publications, 1986.

SPIRITUAL COUNTERFEITS

Pacwa, Rev. Mitch, S.J. *Catholics and the New Age*. Ann Arbor, Mich.: Servant Publications, 1992.

Pontifical Council for Culture; Pontifical Council for Interreligious Dialogue. *Jesus Christ the Bearer of the Water of Life: A Christian Reflection on the "New Age."* February 3, 2003.

Pope Paul VI. Apostolic Exhortation *Evangelii Nuntiandi*. December 8, 1974.

Vatican Congregation for the Doctrine of the Faith. *Instruction on Certain Aspects of "Theology of Liberation."*

Vatican Congregation for the Doctrine of the Faith. *Instruction on Christian Freedom and Liberation*.

OTHER AVAILABLE FAITH FACTS
CREED
All in the Family: The Communion of Saints
Blessed Be God, Father, Son and Holy Spirit
Christ's Descent into Hell
First Marian Dogma: Mary, Mother of God
God's Big Bang: The Church and Evolution
Hell: The Self-exclusion from God
Mary, Conceived without Sin:
    The Dogma of the Immaculate Conception
Mary's Perpetual Virginity
One, Holy, Catholic, and Apostolic:
    The Marks of Christ's Church

Pillar and Bulwark of the Truth:
   The Infallible Magisterium of the Catholic Church
Predestination and Free Will
Private Revelation
Purgatory
Where Do We Go from Here? The Concept of Limbo
What's a Mother to Do? Mary's Role in Our Salvation

LITURGY

Approved Bible Translations for Use at Mass
Bread and Wine Used in Consecration of Eucharist
Church's Norms for Cremation
Come, Worship the Lord! Promoting Adoration
   of the Most Holy Eucharist
Communion Services
Defending Our Rites: Constructively Dealing
   with Liturgical Abuse
Eucharistic Consecration: Kneeling or Standing?
First Confession / First Communion
General Absolution
Is Missing Mass a Mortal Sin?
Invalid Masses
Lay Preaching
Norms for Confession
Reception of Holy Communion
Self-Communication
Signs of the Christ: The Sacraments of the Catholic Church
What Must Be Done for a Valid Baptism?

CHRISTIAN LIVING

All You Need Is Love: The Theological Virtue of Charity
The Book on Gambling
Christian Stewardship: What God Expects from Us
Going God's Way: The Church's Teaching on Moral
Conscience
Here I Am, Lord: Vocations in Christ
Hope: A Pilgrim's Virtue
Human Suffering: Why Does God Permit It?
Proclaiming the Good News to the World:

The Church's Evangelizing Mission
The Theological Virtue of Faith
Ways and Means: Using Today's Technology
    to Evangelize the World

LIFE ISSUES
Be Fruitful and Multiply: The Morality of Fertility Drugs
Canonical Misconception: Pope Pius IX and
    the Church's Teaching on Abortion
Choose Life, That You and Your Children May Live:
    The Truth about Birth Control
The Principle of Double Effect
Reproductive Technologies
True Compassion for the Dying:
    The Church's Teaching on Euthanasia
Withholding Nutrition and Hydration:
    Influences of the Culture of Death

MARRIAGE AND FAMILY ISSUES
Catholic Traditions for Advent and Christmas
Chastity Begins at Home:
    Parental Rights and Chastity Education
Divorce and Remarriage: The Church's Perspective
Lenten Traditions within the Home
Male and Female He Created Them:
    The Church and "Same-Sex Marriages"
Marriage in God's Plan: Discovering the Power of Marital Love
Pure Biology? Effective Chastity Education
Raising Tomorrow's Saints: The Catholic Education of Youth

BIBLICAL APOLOGETICS
Eat, Drink, and Be Catholic:
    The Biblical Prohibition of Eating Blood
Give It a Rest: Sunday Is the Lord's Day
I Confess: Biblical Basis for the Sacrament of Reconciliation
It Works for Me: The Church's Teaching on Justification
Honor Thy Mother: Praising Mary and the Saints
Making "Sense" Out of Scripture:
    The Four Best-Kept Secrets in Biblical Studies Today
No Bull: Papal Authority and Our Response

Persevering to the End: The Biblical Reality of Mortal Sin
Rock Solid: The Salvation History of the Catholic Church
Sola Scriptura? Not According to the Bible
St. Augustine's Real Faith in the Real Presence
Taking God at His Word:
    A Catholic Understanding of Biblical Inerrancy
This Is My Body: Christ's Real Presence in the Eucharist
Why Not Women Priests?

SPIRITUAL CONTERFEITS
All Hallow's Eve
Apocalypse Not Now: The Church, The Millennium, and the Rapture
Can Catholics Be Freemasons?
God or Goddess: Our Heavenly Father Knows Best
We Have but One Teacher, Jesus Christ: Catechesis in our Time
Where Do We Go Wrong? Top Ten Errors in Catechesis Today

To obtain these FAITH FACTS or for a complete list of FAITH FACTS on other topics, call 1-800 MY-FAITH, or visit our Web site: www.cuf.org.

EFFECTIVE LAY WITNESS PROTOCOL

They [the laity] are, by [reason of the] knowledge, competence or outstanding ability which they may enjoy, permitted and sometimes even obliged to express their opinion on those things which concern the good of the Church. When occasions arise, let this be done through the organs erected by the Church for this purpose. Let it always be done in truth, in courage and in prudence, with reverence and charity toward those who by reason of their sacred office represent the person of Christ.[1]

To assist the faithful when controversies arise, the Church has given certain procedures that should be used. These procedures respect the "institutions established by the Church," and are provided for in the Code of Canon Law. There are three types of procedures that can be used: judicial, administrative, and pastoral. In all circumstances, the Church favors pastoral means as a way of resolving disputes.[2] Judicial and administrative recourse should only take place when pastoral means have been exhausted, or the nature of the matter requires immediate and formal action.

Guidelines that Apply to Every Step
A. Pray. Seek the Wisdom of God. Follow the example of the saints and seek their intercession.

B. Know the issue. Study Church documents and other writings on the topic. Our FAITH FACTS are a helpful starting point.

---

[1] Second Vatican Council, Dogmatic Constitution on the Church *Lumen Gentium* (November 21,1964), no. 37.
[2] Cf. *Code of Canon Law* (Washington, D.C.: Canon Law Society of America, 1983), cann. 1446, 1676, 1713–16, 1733.

They provide relevant citations and a list of sources that can be used for further study. The National Conference of Catholic Bishops (NCCB) has various offices that can provide information on their topic of expertise. Its outreaches include offices on Liturgy, Doctrine, and Canonical Affairs. Information from one of these offices can be obtained by writing to the following address: (Name of the Office), United States Conference of Catholic Bishops, 3211 Fourth St., N.E., Washington, DC 20017-1194. Use this information to objectively and prayerfully consider the statements made by those with whom you are in conflict. The Apostolic Pro-nuncio also employs a staff to help answer questions. The address is below.

C. The Church presumes good faith unless otherwise proven. You must do the same, always in charity giving others the benefit of the doubt (cf. Catechism, no. 2478). A contrary approach may jeopardize your ability to obtain an acceptable solution. At all times concisely speak the truth in love (cf. Eph. 4:15), and strive to be an instrument of healing and reconciliation (cf. 2 Cor. 5:18–20).

D. Keep copies of all written materials that pertain to the issue, including letters and decrees. Maintain objective, written records of any meetings, and provide copies of these records to those who participate.

E. The Church favors the principle of subsidiarity. That means issues are to be resolved at the lowest level possible. Always exhaust the possibility of resolution at the lowest level before moving to the next. Do not involve people who are not a part of the solution.

F. During your first contact with higher authority, make him aware of the materials available that pertain to the issue. If possible, provide him with copies of these materials during this first contact. Without these materials, he cannot objectively consider your request.

Pastoral Procedures

A. As a general rule at each level noted below, allow at least two weeks and no more than thirty days for the person you contact to respond to your request before contacting them again. After contacting them a second time with no response, move to the next level.

B. Contact the person with whom you have conflict. Discuss your concerns and seek a mutually agreeable resolution. Do not hesitate to meet more than once. Only when it becomes evident that no mutual solution will be reached, move to the next level of authority as noted below in "C" (cf. Mt. 18:15–17).

C. If the first step does not provide a resolution, contact the immediate superior of the person you are in conflict with. If the person is an employee of the parish, approach the pastor. If the person is a teacher, contact the principal before approaching the pastor.

D. If the person is the pastor, or if you have already contacted the pastor without success, approach the dean of your deanery once. He does not have direct authority over the pastor in most circumstances, but he can act as mediator, and in limited instances he can directly intervene.[3]

E. If the dean is unable to help, find out if your diocese has an office of mediation. The purpose of this office is to assist the faithful in finding agreeable solutions to disputes. The dean can direct you to the office of mediation, if one is available.

F. If the office of mediation is unable to assist you in obtaining an agreeable solution, or if your diocese does not have an office of mediation, approach the bishop or one of his vicars according to diocesan protocol. In larger dioceses, particularly those with an archbishop, it is proper to approach a vicar before approaching the bishop. All dioceses have a vicar general. The

---

[3] Cf. *Code of Canon Law*, cann. 553–55.

larger dioceses also have episcopal vicars, who are often bishops. These vicars have direct authority over the priests entrusted to their care. After approaching the vicar, seek the assistance of the bishop himself.

G. If the bishop is unable to help, contact the archbishop of your ecclesiastical province once. The archbishop does not have direct authority over the bishop, but he does have an obligation to help resolve disputes and report abuses to the Holy See.[4]

H. After contacting the archbishop without success, contact the Apostolic Nuncio at the following address: Apostolic Nuncio, 3339 Massachusetts Ave. N.W., Washington, DC 20008.

I. If the above approaches prove fruitless, contact the Holy See. If it becomes necessary to take this final step, proper procedures must be used and the matter directed to the proper dicastery (office) of the Holy See, or your request will not be addressed. To obtain assistance in taking this step, contact Information Services at (800) 693-2484. If we are unable to help you directly, we will refer you to competent persons who can.

Judicial and Administrative Procedures

A. The Church has the exclusive right to judge cases concerning spiritual matters or connected with spiritual matters, particularly those cases that involve violations of ecclesiastical laws, the culpability of sin, and the imposition of ecclesiastical penalties.[5]

B. The purposes of judicial trials within the Church are: to prosecute or vindicate rights, declare juridic facts (e.g.: whether a marriage took place), and impose or declare penalties.[6]

---

[4] Cf. *Code of Canon Law*, can. 436.
[5] Cf. *Code of Canon Law*, can. 1401.
[6] Cf. *Code of Canon Law*, can. 1400 §1.

C. The purpose of administrative recourse is to settle controversies that arise from acts of administration within the Church.[7]

D. Both judicial and administrative procedures require specific steps in a particular order. Certain time limits must be followed. If the necessary steps or time limits are not followed, a case can be thrown out.

E. Judicial trials are handled by the diocesan tribunal. Administrative procedures begin by contacting the person whose act caused the controversy. Further appeals must follow the designated procedure.

Canonical advocacy is highly recommended if you need to use judicial or administrative procedures. Catholics United for the Faith does not provide canonical advocacy, but we can refer you to competent persons who do. If you are uncertain as to what course of action to follow, call Information Services (800) 693-2484, and we will assist you in determining the best way to proceed.

Important Note

If you are uncertain as to what course of action to follow, call Information Services (800) 693-2484, and we can help you determine the best course of action. If judicial or administrative recourse is necessary, we will refer you to competent persons who can assist you.

If a problem remains unresolved despite following this protocol, resist the temptation to speak uncharitably, which will only aggravate the problem. Offer any difficulties as a sacrifice in union with our Eucharistic Lord for your salvation and for the good of the Church. As the late Mother Teresa taught, we are called to be faithful, not successful. Therefore, never grow weary of doing the right thing (cf. 2 Thess. 3:13). Maintain respect for both the person and office of the sacred pastors of the Church, for they act in the Person of Christ. It is this genuine fidelity to Christ and His Church that is most effective in fostering authentic renewal. As the fathers of Vatican II explained:

---

[7] Cf. *Code of Canon Law*, can. 1400 §2.

Each individual layman must stand before the world as a witness to the resurrection and life of the Lord Jesus and a symbol of the living God. All the laity as a community and each one according to his ability must nourish the world with spiritual fruits. They must diffuse in the world that spirit which animates the poor, the meek, the peace makers—whom the Lord in the Gospel proclaimed as blessed. In a word, "Christians must be to the world what the soul is to the body."[8]

---

[8] Second Vatican Council, *Lumen Gentium*, no. 38, citations omitted.

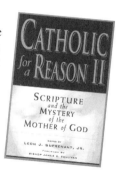